# The Greatest Dad

God's Loving Answer

to the Fatherless

Millie Hull

Forward Light Publications
The Greatest Dad
Copyright© 2013 by Millie Hull

Requests for information should be addressed to:
Forward Light Publications, Taunton, MA 02780

**Library of Congress Cataloging-in-Publication Data**
Hull, Millie
The Greatest Dad
Christian Non-Fiction
Library of Congress Catalog Number:
ISBN: 978-0-578-10379-2

All Scripture quotations in this publication are taken from The Holy Bible, New International Version, ©1973, 1978, 1984 by International Bible Society.
Excerpt from Corrie ten Boom's "Tramp for the Lord" was used by permission of the publisher.
Author's Photo by: Tara Renaud, Photographer
To view her photographs see: www.freshfacephotos.com

Illustrations by: Millie Hull – see www.forward-light-publications.com

Names and places have been changed to protect the privacy of the contributors. Illustrations are of friends and family who posed for the sketches, and are in no way associated with the stories.

All rights reserved. No part of this publication may be reproduced, stored in a retrieval system, or transmitted in any form or by any means – electronic, mechanical, photocopy, recording, or any other – except for brief quotations in printed reviews, without the prior permission of the publisher.

Printed in the United States of America

# Dedication

I dedicate this book to Dominick who had the courage to come forth with his story, knowing that it would help others. It is also dedicated to all the children and adults who do not have earthly fathers. But, most of all, I dedicate this book to my wonderful God, who has become *my greatest Dad!*

# Prayer

Lord, I pray for all the fatherless children, youth, and adults in our world. I pray that they will come to understand that you are waiting to welcome them, with loving, open arms. Please help them come to know you as *their* greatest Dad. Bless them, protect them and help them to become wonderful men and women of God. Lead them in your ways, and draw them close to you. Please help them to become lights shining in the darkness. In Jesus' name, amen.

# Acknowledgments

I'd like to take this time to thank my husband, without whose support, this book could not have been written. You're a great dad and a wonderful husband, and I love you very much. A big thank you to my prayer partner, Joyce Reed. Without your prayer support, Joyce, this book would not have been written. I'd like to thank my Renaissance Women's Group for all their help, encouragement and loving advice. Thanks also to Jeanne Richard and all those who have helped and encouraged me at the Taunton Public Library. Thank you to my daughter, Angela, who helped me greatly with contacts for the stories and to my daughter, Chrissy, who encourages me to continue writing. Thanks to Photographer, Tara Renaud, for her wonderful photo skills in making me look presentable. An enormous thank you to my friend, Lynn Wheaton, who spent many hours styling this book and helping me with technical computer problems. I must also thank my friend, Veda Shibilo for her great editing skills, her time and willingness to help. I am also grateful to my church, Liberty Christian Center. You folks have supported me in an awesome way, and I am forever thankful for that. I also want to thank all those who posed for the sketches in this book. Much appreciation to all of the people who so graciously sat with me and told me their stories. It wasn't easy for you, but you did it in order to help others. God will make those tears we shed together worthwhile. And, most of all, I thank God for his great love. May He bless all of you who made this book possible.

# Table of Contents

Foreword ................................................................. 1
The Greatest Dad ..................................................... 4
Dominick ................................................................ 9
Autumn ................................................................. 13
Willow .................................................................. 19
Sarah .................................................................... 23
Joel ...................................................................... 27
Piper .................................................................... 33
Esther ................................................................... 37
Sienna .................................................................. 43
Luke ..................................................................... 48
Alyssa .................................................................. 54
Paige .................................................................... 62
Grace ................................................................... 70
Dave ..................................................................... 76
Elizabeth .............................................................. 82
Inez ...................................................................... 88
Matt ..................................................................... 94
Arminda ............................................................. 100
Julie .................................................................... 106
Ricardo ............................................................... 112
Daniel ................................................................. 118
Gloria ................................................................. 124
Why Does God Let Bad Things Happen To Us? ...... 128
How Can I Forgive Those Who've Hurt Me? ......... 131
How God Can Become *Your* Greatest Dad .......... 134
A Letter from Your Heavenly Father To You ........ 137
Famous People Who Grew Up Without
    a Father in the Home ..................................... 139
Afterword ........................................................... 141

# Foreword

This book actually started as a poem for a young man named Dominick who attended my church. One night, as I was assisting the teacher of the Youth Group, I said to Dominick, "I saw you with your dad the other day, at Wendy's." Dominick froze at my words, and gave me a withering look. I quickly realized that I had misspoken so I said, "Oh, I meant to say, I saw you with your grandfather." I didn't understand why I had gotten such a strong reaction.

Later, I asked his grandmother what the problem was. She said, "Oh Millie, you couldn't have known, but Dominick's dad died years ago." Well, I was crushed. I couldn't believe I had said such a thing. Of course, as soon as I saw Dominick again, I apologized, but he just gave me another look, grunted, and walked away. So, I went home feeling dejected and angry at myself.

Sometimes, when I am feeling low, writing seems to help, so I sat down and started writing a poem. That's how the poem, "The Greatest Dad," was born. When I finished the poem and reread it, I knew it was meant for Dominick. So, I printed it out on some pretty, sky-blue paper with clouds on it. The following week, I gave it to his grandmother to give to him. She did so, but I never heard anything about it again. Three months later, I asked his grandmother what Dominick thought of the poem. I said, "He's never mentioned it, and he still doesn't speak to me." His grandmother smiled and said, "Millie, although he never thanked you for that poem, he framed it, and keeps it on the bureau beside his bed."

After that, God impressed upon me that the poem was not just a poem – that it was to be part of a book. The book was not just for Dominick, but for everyone who grew up without a dad. When I realized that, I began writing this book.

Dominick is a brave young man who recently sat down with me and talked to me about his father. You will find Dominick and his dad included in this book. Dominick and I were both amazed to find out that I had taught his dad in Sunday School when he was a little boy. Dominick's dad was only 36 years old when he died. I remember him as a sweet little boy with sparkling brown eyes, who loved to laugh and make others laugh. As they say, it's a small world!

And so, this book was written for young people who don't have fathers. This can be due to unwed-mother situations, divorces, separations, deaths, fathers who are incarcerated, and fathers who, for whatever reasons, simply walk away from their families.

I was amazed to find that, according to the U.S. Census Bureau, one third of American children are growing up without their biological father. In the past fifty years, the number of children who live with two married parents has dropped. During that same time, the number of babies born to unwed mothers rose from 5% to 40%. Because I have taught Sunday School for 34 years, I have seen the repercussions of this problem. I felt led by God to write this book for the fatherless of all ages. I want them to know that God loves them and wants to be a father to them. Through this book, I pray that they will come to understand that God is the Greatest Dad!

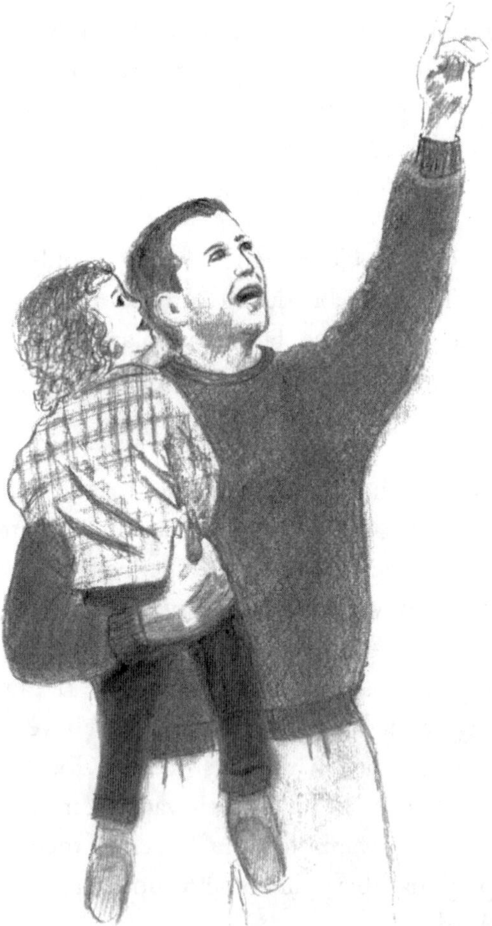

# The Greatest Dad

They say I do not have a dad.
But that's not really so,
Because I have the greatest dad
That you could ever know.

Yes, my dad understands me,
And he knows me very well.
He knows what I am thinking of
Before I even tell.

And my dad goes to all my games.
He's always there for me.
And when I want to talk to him,
He listens carefully.

Dad always takes good care of me.
He gives me all I need.
He shows me how to live my life
When his good Book I read.

And my dad watches over me,
All day and through the night.
He comforts me when I'm afraid
And always makes things right.

My dad is there to heal my heart
Whenever I am sad,
And often sends me someone who
Knows how to make me glad.

I love my dad so very much,
And when I put him first,
He gives me joy so deep and wide,
I feel like I could burst!

And my dad keeps his promises
His word is firm and true.
I want to be just like him and
Be honest through and through.

When I look at the great blue sky,
The clouds, moon, stars and sun,
I praise my dad for all of the
Great works that he has done!

My dad has a great plan for me.
He wants me to succeed.
He's always there to guide my way,
If I learn to let him lead.

When others hurt my feelings and
My heart is full of pain,
He shows me that I must forgive.
He helps me smile again.

And my dad gently shows me when
I do something that's wrong.
Forgiving me when I confess,
He fills my heart with song.

I do not have an earthly dad.
He's gone away you see,
But I do have a Heavenly Dad
Who's always there for me.

If you don't have an earthly dad,
I'll share my dad with you
I know He'd love to be your dad
If you just ask him to.

Millie Hull

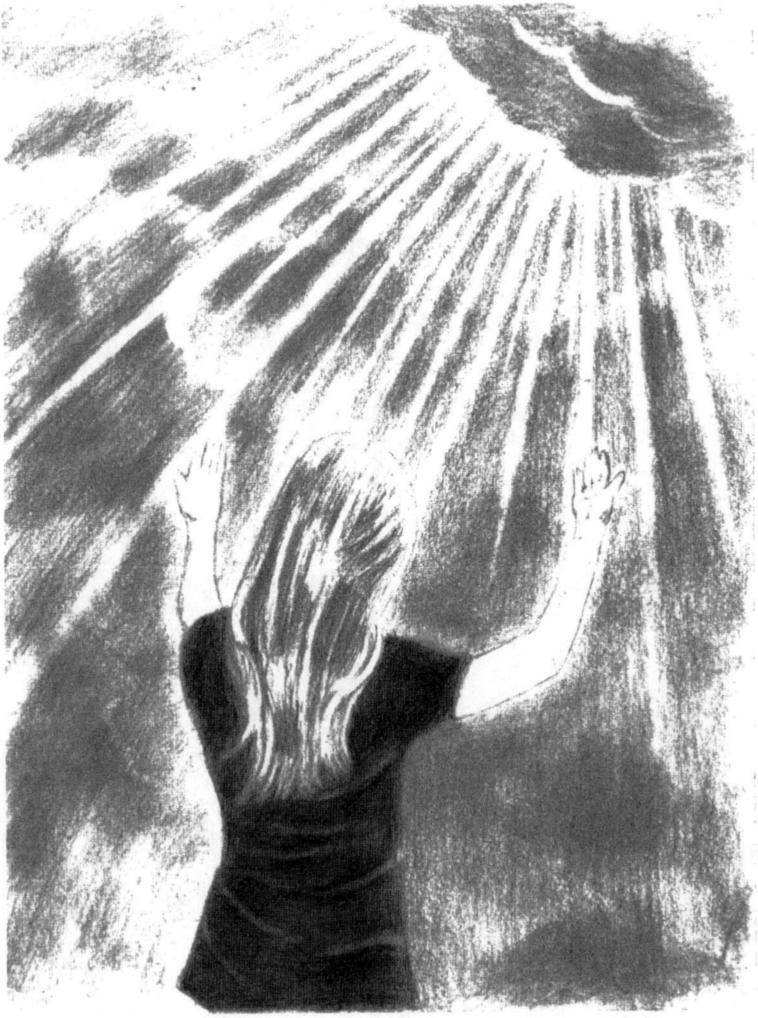

# DOMINICK

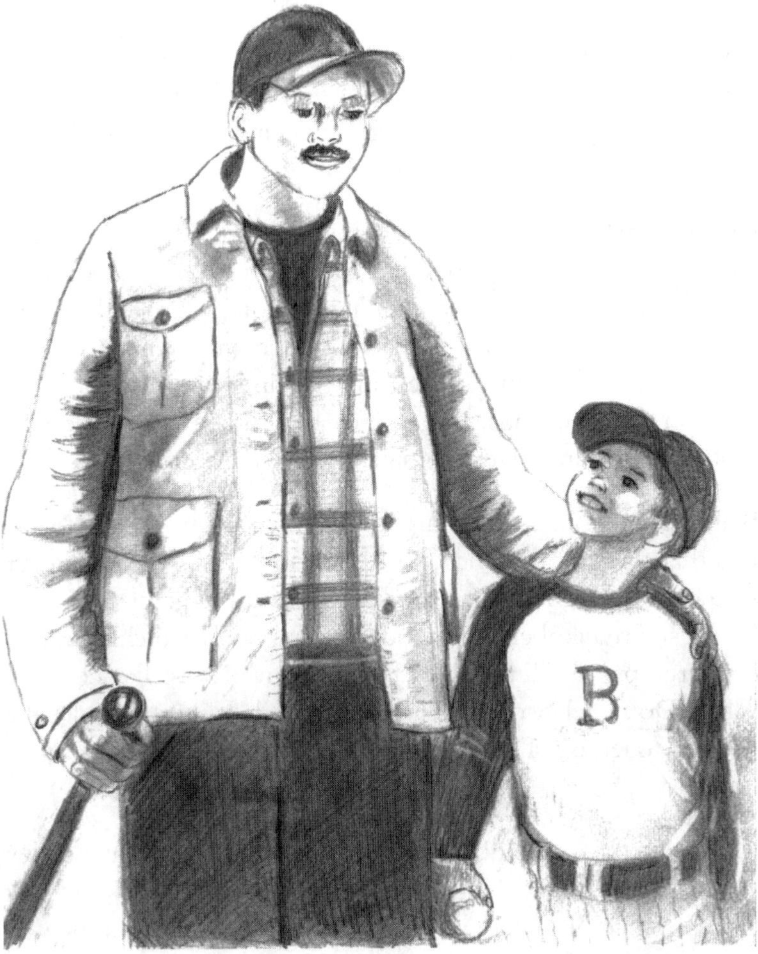
B

# Dominick

*Dominick is a strong, athletic young man who enjoys playing all kinds of sports. His life inspired me to write this book. Dominick loved his father very much, as you will see from his story:*

Savannah Anderson and Blake Bronson were thrilled to welcome their son, Dominick, into the world. Blake came out of the delivery room with a huge smile and announced, "It's a boy!" That was a happy day for them.

Unfortunately, their happiness didn't last. When Dominick was two years old, his mom and dad split up. He had a loving mom and dad but they couldn't get along with each other. Dominick's dad was an excellent father who remained very involved with his son. Blake took the time to have Dominick over on the weekends. And since he worked nights, he also spent his mornings with Dominick, while Savannah worked.

Blake came from a large family of ten children. When Blake was thirty, his mother died, so Blake took over the cooking for all the holidays for his entire family. He was a great cook! His family still remembers his wonderful, fragrant fried chicken and his scrumptious Ziti recipe. He also loved to bake cookies. When Dominick went to stay with his dad, they would bake cookies together. Dominick wistfully remembers the fun they had.

As Dominick grew older, Blake encouraged him to play hockey at the Boys' Club. He attended all of Dominick's hockey games. Since Blake had worked at the Boys' Club when he was sixteen, everyone knew him there. He was very popular. His great sense of humor, sparkling brown eyes, and happy countenance attracted people to him.

Although Savannah and Blake didn't get along, they always came together to provide for their son. Dominick vividly remembers one year, when he was nine or ten, his mom and dad got together and bought him a Play Station II. He hadn't asked for one because he knew it was very expensive, and his folks didn't have lots of money. "I was amazed when I received it!" Dominick said.

When Dominick was eleven, his dad became ill with a liver problem and other complications. Dominick went to the hospital to see his dad, and remembers praying for him with other people. Blake took some time alone with his son, and told him, "I made some stupid decisions, but you grow up to be a good man." Shortly after that, Blake Bronson died, leaving his eleven-year-old son to grieve his loss.

And Dominick did grieve deeply. Depression set in for a long while. Although his mom, Savannah, was there for him, nothing seemed to fill the void of not having a dad.

Dominick is now eighteen. Last year he volunteered at the Boys' Club for the summer, as his own dad had done when he was sixteen. "People there who knew my dad say I look just like him." Dominick says proudly. "They say it's almost like having my dad back." Dominick gave me one of his rare smiles as he said this.

Dominick told me that he accepted Christ in 2008. He said, "Now, I always have someone to talk to. I tell God everything – good or bad."

*Find rest, O my soul, in God alone; my hope comes from him. He alone is my rock and my salvation; he is my fortress. I will not be shaken.*
***PSALM 62: 5***

# AUTUMN

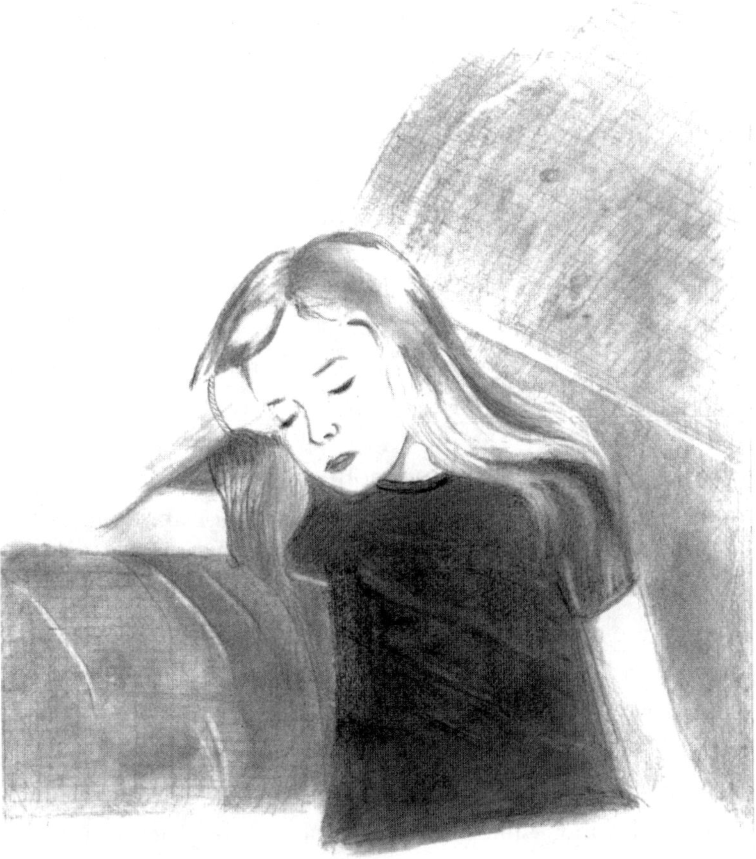

# Autumn

*Autumn is a beautiful woman, inside and out. She loves her children and is a good mother to them. Autumn has been through a lot, and has gained wisdom beyond her years, as you will see from her story:*

My mother and Dad lived in Arizona. They got married very young, and really weren't ready for the responsibilities. It was a funny way that they found out I was going to be born. They thought my mom had a tumor, and so they came to New England to get medical help, and then found out it was a baby, and not a tumor. And so, I was a pleasant surprise to them.

My dad was bipolar but he didn't even know it; he was also an addict. My mother was a very passive woman. It felt like she was more of a sister to me than a mother. There were 3 of us girls and I was the oldest.

One day, my grandfather, my mom and dad got into a fight, so my grandfather called the Department of Social Services, and they took all of us girls out of the home. We were placed in the foster care system. I was placed by myself and my two sisters were placed together. I can't even tell you how many foster homes I was in. I know it was at least ten in one year. It seemed like every month I was moved. At the age of six, I stayed for 4 years in one home. It was the home of a woman and her boyfriend. They had two older kids. The woman was an alcoholic and, while she was drunk, her boyfriend molested me. She drank every day, but she was a very nurturing person, and I even called her Mommy. She liked playing bingo, and when she went to play, I was left alone with her boyfriend.

I had a best friend next door who went to Youth Group, and so I started going to Youth Group and Christian camps with her. That was a good thing, and it helped me a lot. But then, when it was found out by DSS that my foster mother drank, they took me out of that home, placing me and my two sisters with a relative. That situation didn't work out, and we were put back into foster care. We were in many foster homes after that. And then at the age of fifteen, I got an awesome foster mother, who became a real mother to me. She even sent me to Spain. She had me pay for my spending money in Spain by selling candy bars. That taught me good work ethics. I loved being with her, and I am still close to her today.

At the age of sixteen, I went back with my mother. I started hanging out with an eighteen year old man. My mother tried to warn me about him. She knew he wasn't good for me, but I didn't listen. She was right, of course. He drank and took drugs. I soon found out that I was pregnant.

When I found out that I was pregnant, I took off to my father's home. It wasn't what I thought it would be. I had good times with my father, but there was no structure and no guidance. Realizing I needed that, I went back to my mother, continued school, and had my son. I was very happy to have him, as I love children. When he got sick, I quit school and went right to work. I got a job as a secretary, put my child in daycare full time, and got my license with the help of some friends. My dad bought me a car, and I found an apartment to live in. So, at eighteen, I was out of state care, had a full-time job, and an apartment. Things were looking good, but I still had to deal with my son's father. I found out that to get away from a bad situation, I needed to move back with my dad.

In my teens and twenties, I went from relationship to relationship. I had four children out of wedlock, always seeking to fill the void within. My first priority was my children and I wanted to be sure they had a good life. However, in searching for a good husband for me and a good dad for them, I tried to find love in all the wrong places.

I was twenty-seven when I had my fourth child. During this pregnancy, I had postpartum depression and was very ill from it. I felt the need to seek the Lord for help, so I drove myself to a church and sat in a pew. The pastor said that people have voids in their hearts, and that depression and anxiety were symptoms of that void. He said that a relationship with Jesus Christ could fill that void. His words made a lot of sense to me, and so I accepted Jesus as my Savior that day. It changed my life. The depression and anxiety went away, and I was a new person with a new beginning.

As I started growing in the Lord, it was like scales coming off my eyes. As I understood more and more, I realized that God was slowly transforming and molding me to whom I am meant to be. My hurts and wounds of the past are being healed. Today, I am blessed with 7 children and a Godly man I can trust and appreciate. He is a good father to my children, and I thank God for him.

My will is to serve God. I have no ill feeling towards anyone for all the bad things in my past. I know that my parents did the best they could. They've had it tough too.

Even though I continue to experience trials, and tribulations, I see hope and victory on the horizon. As long as I stay in the word and seek Jesus' face, he makes all things possible to me. His grace is sufficient.

One of the biggest problems I faced in life was rejection. It felt like I was always being rejected and I thought that Jesus would reject me too. But He accepted me unconditionally, and he has carried me when my parents couldn't. I thought relationships would carry me, but they couldn't, and Jesus did. Man will fail you, but Jesus never will. He's changed my life, and he can change yours also.

***I love you, O Lord, my strength.***
***The Lord is my rock, my fortress and my deliverer; my God is my rock, in whom I take refuge. He is my shield and the horn of my salvation, my stronghold.***
***Psalm 18:1-2***

# WILLOW

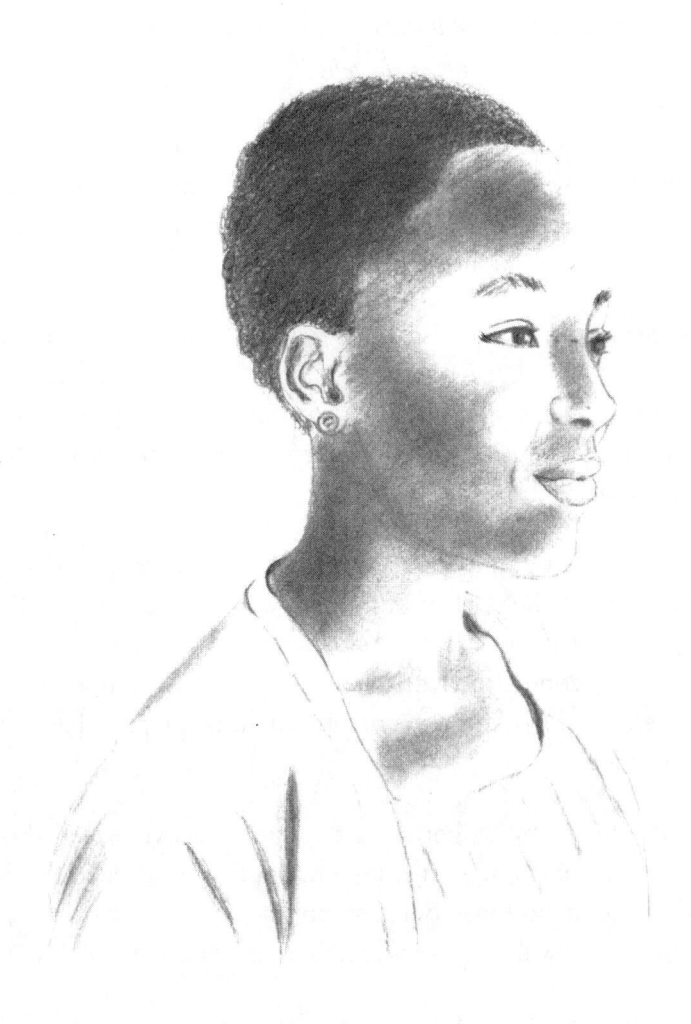

# Willow

*Willow is a very intelligent and sweet young lady who wants to help others, and has dreams of becoming a pediatrician. Here's her story as she tells it:*

My dad was around for about two months after I was born, then he left my mom and me. The relationship between him and my mom wasn't good. I've never met my father, and I don't even have a picture of him.

I miss having a dad. Life isn't easy without one. When I was in elementary school, there was a Father/Daughter Dance. I wanted to go so badly, but I had no one to go with me, so I stayed home and cried. My heart broke each time I saw other girls with their fathers.

As I got older, I graduated high school and accomplished a lot with my mom's help. I wish my dad was here to see that I've become a Certified Nursing Assistant. I love helping people. I'd like to become a pediatric nurse or a pediatrician, so that's the dream I'm working toward. It would be great to have my own practice.

I've tried to find my father using the internet. I've Googled his name, used some search engines, and looked on Facebook. So far I've found nothing, but I'm optimistic. Someday, I hope that maybe he will search for me. You never know.

I've learned a lot from my parents' situation. I'm definitely going to get married before I have children and I will also wait until I'm older to do it. I think about the future and I think about marriage. If I never find my dad, who will walk me down the aisle when I get married?

A friend of mine mentioned that since I don't know what my dad looks like, I could possibly walk right by him and never know it. It's sad to think about it, but it's true. One time a man, whom I didn't know, spoke to me at Wendy's. He told me that I reminded him of his daughter. That made me wonder… Could he be my dad? Now, anytime I walk by a man who looks a little like me, I wonder…

>  ***Be strong and take heart,***
>  ***All you who hope in the Lord.***
>  ***PSALM 31:24***

# SARAH

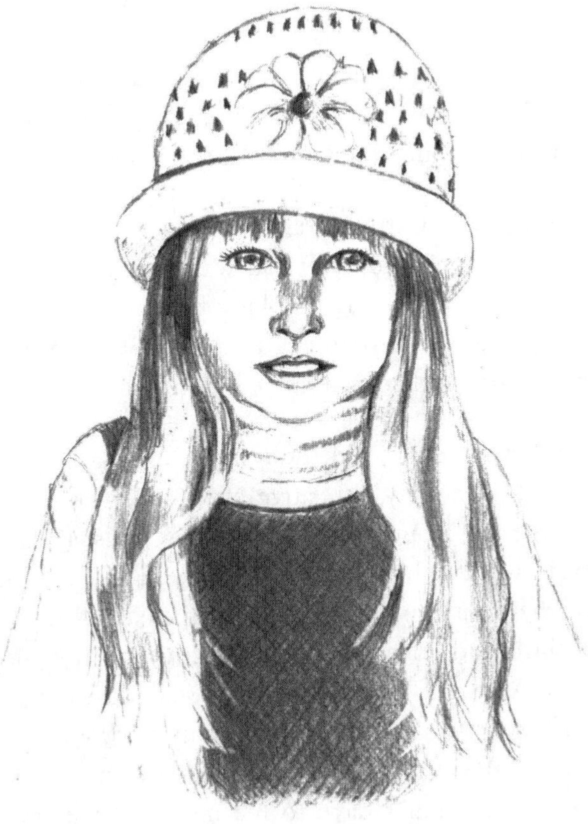

# Sarah

*Sarah is vivacious and sweet natured. She is the type of person you like immediately. This is her story:*

My mom and dad were very good parents. I was the middle child of eight children, and we were like the Brady Bunch. Dad was full of life and took us everywhere. There were so many of us, and yet he was close to us all. Although Mom and Dad cared very much for us, I felt a bit lost in the crowd, and always wished that I could have more time with my dad. I didn't have a lot of one-to-one time with him, and I missed that.

Dad and Mom were Catholics and had a strong faith. They taught us to love the Lord. My dad was a strict father, and I was a little bit afraid of him. Looking back, though, it was a good thing because it kept me out of trouble. Dad was a workaholic, a hard worker, and he provided well for his family.

When I was seventeen and in the last year of high school my dad became ill. One day, a relative came and picked my two sisters and me up from school. That was unusual, and she didn't explain why. When we arrived home, I saw lots of cars in front of the house, and suddenly, my stomach turned over, and I felt a little nauseous. I knew instinctively that something was wrong. We went in and someone said, "Your mother's upstairs." As soon as I entered the room, and saw that my father wasn't in the bed and the bed was made up, I knew my dad had died. She didn't have to tell me. I just knew. She said, "Everything is going to be all right. We have our faith. "She was grieving, but in control – a very strong person.

We found out later that my father had choked to death. We all grieved over his death. It affected me physically, for about a year, but we carried on. My mother was an incredible woman. After my father's death, she took care of eight children, and was still able to take over my father's business. She ran it so successfully that we still have it today. My youngest sister was still a baby when my father died, and yet Mom managed to hold things together. None of us kids ever got into trouble or into drugs. Whatever happened, she always said, "We have to turn to God."

I was one of the fortunate ones, to have such a fine father, but to lose him at seventeen was a blow to me. That's when you really need a dad. I didn't know how to relate to men because I lost my dad so early. It affected my confidence, but as my mother told me to do, I turned to God.

We all want unconditional love and support from our fathers. Even when we have a wonderful father, it's impossible to have that because our earthly father is only human, and he can't be perfect. Only God can provide the unconditional love that we all desire. Only God can be there for us whenever we need him.

*You are my God, and I will give you thanks;*
*You are my God, and I will exalt you.*
*Give thanks to the Lord, for he is good;*
*His love endures forever.*
*Psalm 118:28-29*

# JOEL

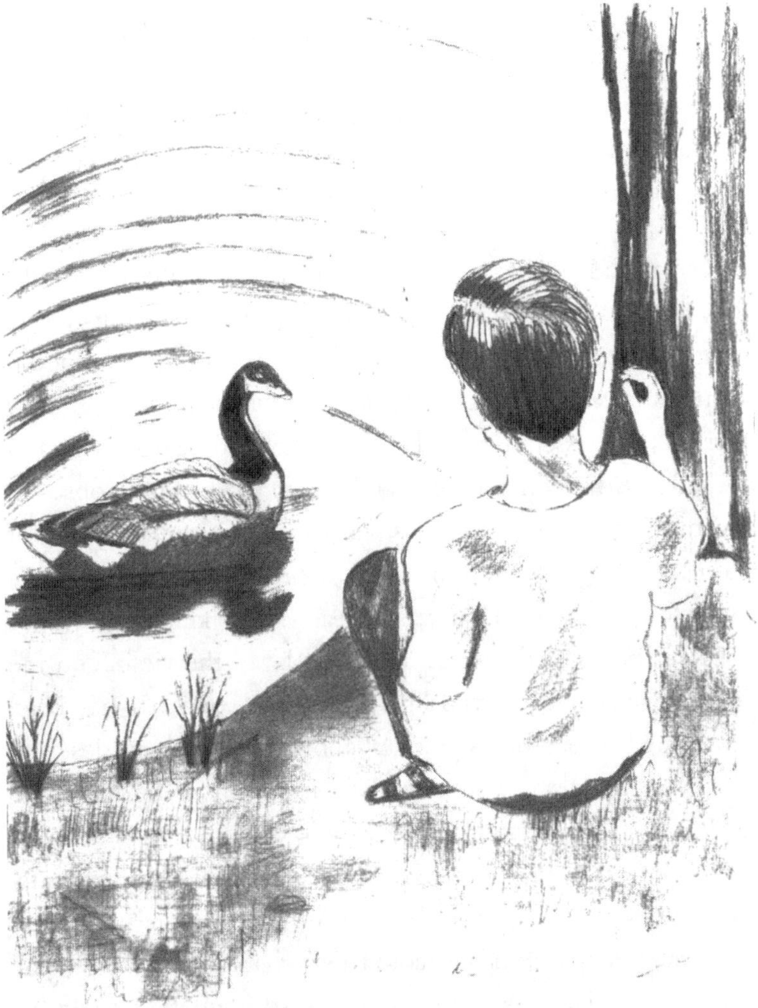

# Joel

*I don't know Joel very well, but from what I've seen, he loves his wife, children and grandchildren very much. Joel is a man of many talents — a good writer and artist, and has retired from two prominent positions. Here's his story, as he tells it:*

A dollar doesn't mean much today, and its value can't take you very far. But a dollar has special meaning in my life. This story will explain why.

My mom and dad were born in Brava, Cape Verde Islands. They came to this country and got married and lived in Rhode Island. They had four sons, and I was second to the youngest. Mom was previously married and had two children from that marriage, my sister and my brother. My dad was a cook, and worked at a diner in Rhode Island. Mom worked two jobs — as a seamstress, as well as a housekeeper. My sister took care of the rest of us. This was during the depression and things were tough for everyone. Dad was an easy-going kind of guy. He loved his booze and music. He also played the violin and the viola. I still have his viola hanging in my den. It has been refurbished several times, but still contains aged memories. On Sundays, my dad would make his rounds through the neighborhood collecting numbers. It was the old version of today's lottery. Back then, you could bet a nickel, dime, etc. The winning numbers were based on the horse races and their outcome. People said you could tell what time it was by my dad's route. He was a consistent person and you could set your watch by him. At other times, you could find him mingling with friends at the local barbershop. Friday night was music and dancing night at a local gathering place. You would find him there with his cigarette dangling from his mouth, and a shot glass next to him, while he and his fellow musicians played on through the night.

I was five years old when my mom carted all six of us kids to Massachusetts. My dad was reluctant to go as he preferred Rhode Island which is where most of our family resided. My mom's older sister and other relatives lived in Massachusetts where there were more opportunities for work in the garment industry. My dad preferred the more tranquil setting where we lived in Rhode Island, but he decided he would give it a shot. Well, that lasted about two years and then my dad and mom split up. My dad went back to Rhode Island.

After that, each Christmas, my dad would send each of us kids a card with a dollar in it – no note or message, just a dollar. He sent us the dollar every Christmas until our very early teens. After that, we were on our own. To make a living, we sold newspapers and shined shoes on the fishing docks. During cranberry season you would find us working the cranberry bogs. We sometimes even squashed grapes in our neighbor's basement during wine-making season. As we grew older, we eventually worked delivering coal, ice and kerosene to homes. My parents never got back together again and my brothers and I eventually went out to sea. I got married in 1955, and my wife and I moved to New Hampshire. A year later, we had our first son.

Sometime after that, my dad was hospitalized due to a problem with his liver, which then affected his heart. I could not get away to see him at that time, but I did plan to go see him during the Thanksgiving holidays. Before I could go, he was released from the hospital. Shortly afterwards, he collapsed on the steps of the nearby Portuguese Catholic Church and died. I regretted that I had never gotten to know my dad. I also regretted the fact that he never got to know my son.

The dollar and the card perhaps don't seem like much to you, but to me it proves that he remembered. My dad was not a man of means or ambition. He died with $3.00 to his name, and left very little for us to understand of his life. I will never know my dad's inner thoughts, but I guess he did the best he knew how to do.

My life, as much as I would have liked it to be, has not been as Robert Young played the part in "Father Knows Best". I've been married three times, and my four children have suffered for it. Parenting is not something that you can go to school and learn. You learn it by example. Unfortunately, I didn't have a great example to go by. I haven't always been there for my kids, and I'm sorry for that. I've been trying to make up for the lost time with my children now.

I married my third wife thirteen years ago, and she is my angel. She is always there for me, and has really helped me maintain a good relationship with my kids. My children have accepted her, and they admire her greatly. She has been a good influence in my life and has taught me the meaning of unconditional love.

I'm trying to be there for my kids now and to have a good relationship with them. I'm determined to communicate with my children, instead of avoiding communication as my father did with his.

I want my kids to know that I love them very much, and that I want to be there for them now.

> ***I will be a Father to you and you will be my sons and daughters, says the Lord Almighty.***
> ***II Corinthians 6:18***

# PIPER

# Piper

*Piper is a cute young girl, who is funny, intelligent, and loves to dance. Here's her story as she tells it:*

I'm not exactly the story you're looking for,* but I do not have a father in my life. My parents divorced when I was two years old. Dad remarried and moved away. I vaguely remember playing tag with my dad when I was really little, but that's about it. Yes, he's still alive. Yes, he calls on Christmas, New Years, and my birthday. No I do not see him, and haven't since seventh grade. I saw him for two weeks every summer between the ages of three through eight. When I was nine, I went to live with him because things weren't going too well between me and my mom at the time. That was a bad idea. My dad had a new family and it didn't work out there. Things got so bad that I was put into two centers. At the end of fifth grade I got a foster home. That was awesome. I had a mother and father, three sisters and one brother. I loved them very much and still do. Into the second month of sixth grade, my mother finally got me back. After getting back with my mom, everyday things got better and better.

I never talked to anyone about my problems until I met my friends Emily and Collin. They understood and supported me. I was closest to Collin as he was in the same situation as I was. If I could ever see them again I would say thank you and I love you.

*Note from the author: Yes, Piper, yours is just the kind of story I'm looking for – a story where the contributor cares about others, and wants to help them, a story told from the heart. Thank you!*

I'm sorry that this is all I've got for you. I'm not the right or perfect story you're looking for. My story is pain, hope, fear and faith. Every time I cried, I would say to myself, "Shut up; it's gonna be ok. Someone out there is worse than you."

I want people to know that everybody is hurting in different ways. Please know that you're not alone. Yes, what I'd really like you to know is that if someone else can make it through, so can you!

> ***But you O God do see trouble and grief;***
> ***you consider it to take it in hand.***
> ***The victim commits himself to you;***
> ***you are the helper of the fatherless.***
> ***Psalm 10:14***

# ESTHER

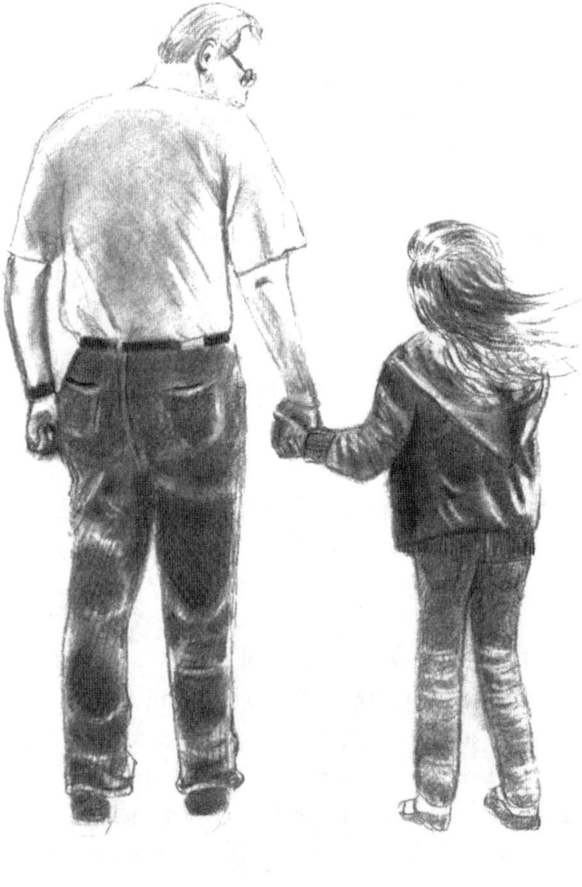

# Esther

*Esther is a very sweet lady who loves people and wants to make others happy. I'm privileged to have her as a friend. Here's her story, in her own words:*

I was nine years old and in the fourth grade when my dad died. He was only fifty-nine when he suffered a massive coronary. He and I were very close. I was the apple of his eye and he was mine. I couldn't have asked for a better father.

The night before he died, they woke me up out of a sound sleep and said, "You have to say goodbye to Daddy. He's sick and going to the hospital. Dad may have asked to see me, I don't know, or maybe it was someone else's idea. But, I'm glad I did see him. They took me into the room where he sat in a rocking chair. I sat in his lap and hugged him. I was very upset that he was sick, but I didn't really understand how sick he was. I don't think anybody did. That night, he went to the hospital and I went back to bed. It was the last time I saw my dad alive.

The next day, they sent me to school. It was probably just around lunch time when my aunt picked me up in her car. That was unusual, as I always walked home for lunch. We drove home and there were lots of cars in the driveway. I asked my aunt what was wrong and she told me that my dad had died. I was stunned, but I really didn't understand what that meant.

I don't remember a lot of what happened after that. I do remember sitting in a chair, looking up at the priest in his black suit and white collar. He tried to comfort me. My mother was crying and wailing in the other room. I don't remember anyone except the priest trying to comfort me. They were all too buried in their own grief to even think about me.

My memories are very sketchy. I remember going to the wake, and looking down into the coffin and breaking down in tears. They took me away after that. No one explained anything to me. I was so confused. Later, I was asked if I wanted to go to the funeral and I said no, so I didn't go. I'm sorry about that now. My teacher and all the children in my fourth grade class went to the funeral, and I wasn't there. I should have gone. But we can't go back and change things.

At the age of nine, I didn't really understand death. I remember one day, when I was getting ready to go to confession, Mom said, "Debbie's here." I thought she said Daddy's here, and I ran into the room saying "Daddy! Daddy!"

Another time I saw a man who looked like my dad and I ran to him saying, "There he is! There he is!", only to find that it wasn't my dad at all...

I do have wonderful memories of my dad. He took me on car rides. First he would buy me penny candy and then he'd ask me where I wanted to go. I'd say, "Bring me to the hills!" and he would take me to the hills of Fall River. I thought it was as exciting as a roller coaster ride to zoom in the car over those hills. My dad also would take me on walks. He often went on errands to buy bread, and he would take me with him. He would always buy me a jelly donut. Or sometimes we would just walk around the block together. When we'd get home, he would twirl a rope for me so I could jump rope. He showed his love for me in so many ways! I'll never forget my dad!

This may sound like a sad story, but it's really a happy one because my dad was so loving and giving. Because of the way my dad was to me, it was easy for me to understand the concept of a loving Heavenly Father. And because of the way things were when my dad died, I am more sensitive to people's needs today. I always try to make sure that other people's feelings are not hurt and try to give comfort when I can.

> ***But I trust in your unfailing love;***
> ***my heart rejoices in your salvation.***
> ***I will sing to the Lord,***
> ***for he has been good to me.***
> ***Psalm 13:5-6***

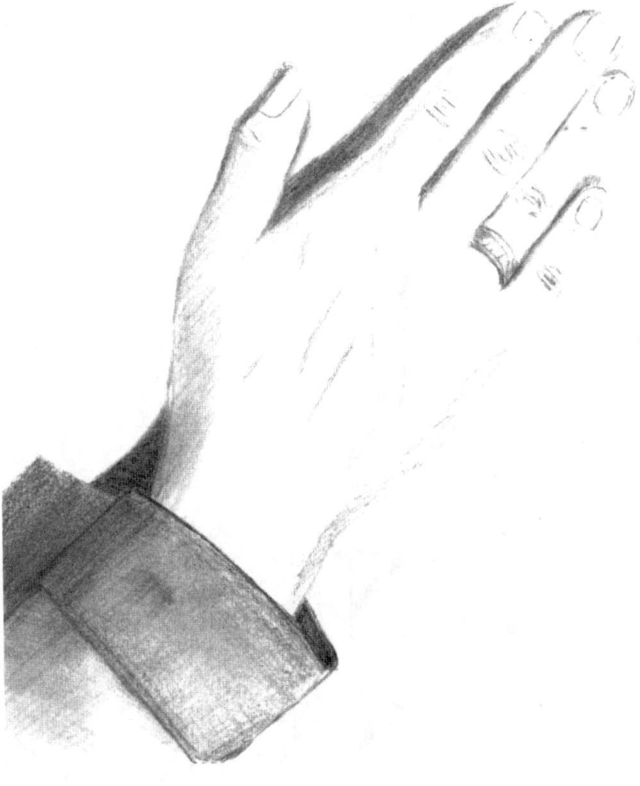

# SIENNA

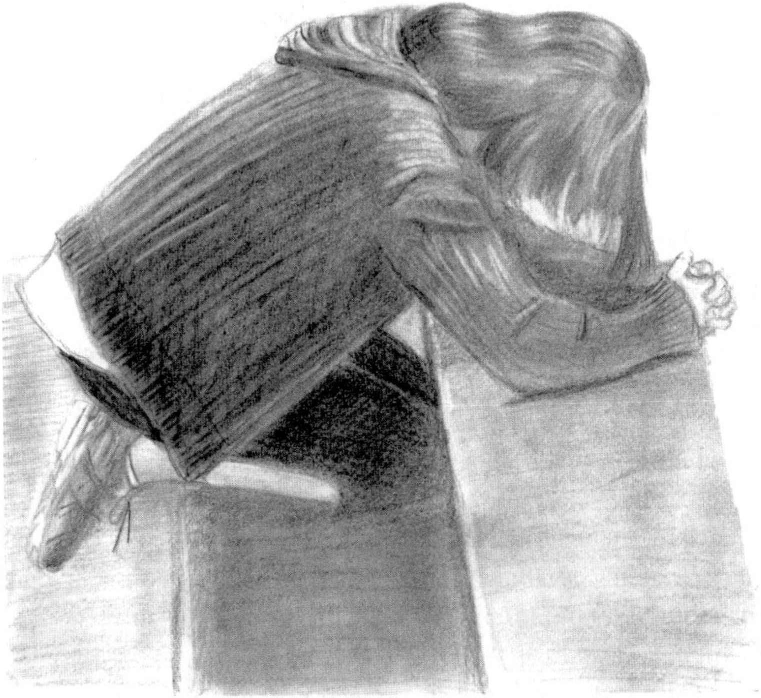

# Sienna

*Sienna is cheerful, funny, and always willing to help others. She loves God very much, and wants to serve him. This is her story:*

My childhood, from when I was a baby to my teenage years, was filled with lots of violence. I've been told that it was a miracle that I survived. Yes, it was pretty horrible, but God had his hand on me even before I knew Him. I'm glossing over a lot of what happened because I've forgiven those people who hurt me, and I don't want to open up old wounds.

When I was in high school, I met my friend, Alexis. She invited me to church and I went. I was in the first stage of being Goth, was depressed, angry, and had attempted suicide a couple of times. I'm not proud of that, but I did make a good decision to give church a try. I thought to myself, here I am, a Goth chick, and I'm going to church! Unbelievable!

The first person I met at the church was an usher named Mr. B. He told me, "It's okay, don't be scared; you can come in." It was a new environment for me and I really *was* scared. I found my friend, Alexis, as quickly as I could, and stayed glued to her side. I became a pew warmer for a few years, but then the church people started a new program called "Fan the Flames". It was for young adults, and everyone had a job to do. I worked the overhead projector, and I also sang in the choir. This program brought me closer to God.

One day, the church showed the movie, The Passion of the Christ. It really moved me, but I was still kind of dead to spiritual things. Slowly, I got closer to God. It took a long time. Because I really had a hard time trusting people, I also had a hard time trusting God.

One year, I became very sick and I said, "God, why am I so sick?" I couldn't breathe as I was all stuffed up; I couldn't sleep, and I had dark circles around my eyes like a raccoon. I kind of ranted and raved at God for letting me get so sick. Well, I fell asleep with a cough drop in my mouth and had a dream. In the dream, I was at the gates of hell and the flames were trying to pull me in. I heard a voice say, "She's my bride. You're not taking her!" Then I immediately woke up. I found that the cough drop was stuck in my throat and I *really* couldn't breathe. I leaned forward, coughed, and the cough drop came out of my throat.

I told someone at church what had happened, and they said, "God was speaking to you." I know that he was. That dream helped me see that God did really love me, and so I decided that I would live for him and serve him.

Then came a day when things got so bad at home that I *had* to leave. I didn't know where to go or what to do. That's when my friend Alexis's family took me in. I cried for a half hour, but then the peace of God came over me. It was like a weight was taken off of me.

So, when I went to live with Alexis, I gained a family. I am so grateful to them for taking me in. I also have a church family and a family where I work.

I'm not afraid anymore. I know that God is my Father, and he loves me and he will take good care of me. I realize that God sent his Son to die for me. Imagine God loving me *that much*?

**Lo, I am with you always.**
**I will never leave you nor forsake you.**
**Hebrews 13: 5**

# LUKE

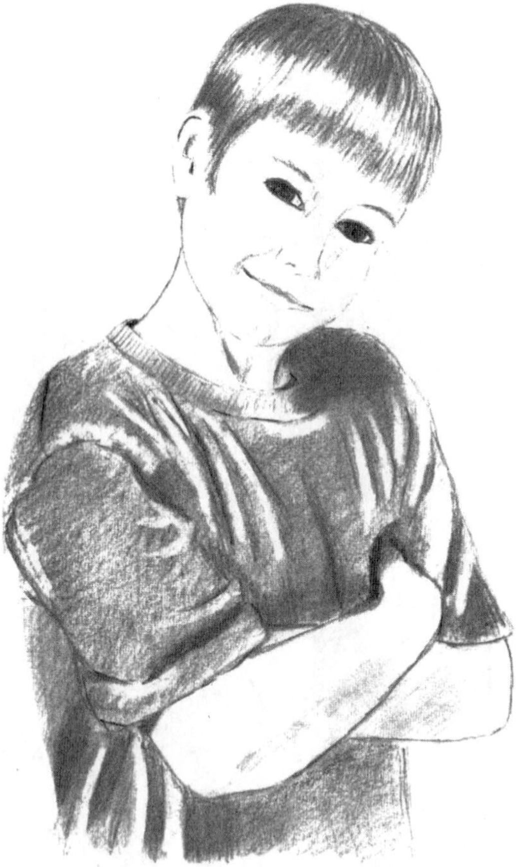

# Luke

*Luke is full of fun and laughter. You can't be serious around him for very long. Here's his story as he told it to me:*

My dad died when he was only forty-two, and I was nine years old. He died just after Thanksgiving, of Pancreatic Cancer. He was a wonderful father, and I loved him. I was the youngest of nine children. We were brought up well, with each one of us having our own chores to do. We had to help out since my parents both worked.

We had lots of funny times with my dad. I remember one day when my older twin brothers and I were given the job of taking out the trash. We were supposed to burn it in the fire pit outside. My dad carefully explained to us that we were to sort out the trash, burn the papers, and put aside the cans and bottles. While we were doing that, about 15 or 20 feet away, our father began cleaning out the cesspool which was clogged. He took the lid off of it, placed a 2 x 8 plank across the top, and stood on the plank. Then he took a long-handled shovel and proceeded to unclog the cesspool. The fire pit we were using was made of fieldstone, and had cast iron doors. I was helping to sort out the stuff to burn. When I found an aerosol can in there, my brothers told me to throw it in the fire, and so I did. Bad idea! When I threw it in, it exploded, cracked the chimney and the cast iron doors blew open! Everything shook and my dad almost fell into the cesspool. I laughed nervously when that happened and the soot from the chimney got all over my teeth! My mom was out on the porch and saw the whole thing. She laughed uncontrollably at my dad almost falling into the cesspool. I went up on the porch to her, still laughing nervously, and she saw my black teeth. Mom and Dad really cracked up at that! My dad scolded my brothers for doing it, but I didn't get scolded since I was little and only did what they told me to do. I often did crazy things like that, but got away with it. My brothers and sisters called me the king, and my youngest sister the queen because of what we got away with.

My dad was a hard worker. He worked at Reed and Barton Silverware Company, and he also did carpentry around the house. One day, as he was putting up a pantry door, I took his hammer and started breaking up rocks in the stone wall outside. I was having a good time doing it, but Dad didn't approve. He came outside and shouted, "Don't take my hammer and break stones!" My brother loved it that I *finally* got in trouble, and he took a picture of my dad's angry face. I still have that picture today!

Our Dad also told us "Never go across the highway." Across the highway was the cemetery. It had big tombstones everywhere. One day my twin brothers and I went there anyway. When we found half-smoked cigarettes and matches, my brothers started smoking. They thought they were pretty grownup doing that until we spotted my father's two-toned blue, Ford Fairlane coming down the road. We quickly hid so he wouldn't see us. My brothers hastily got rid of the cigarettes and we went back home.

When we got to the driveway, my father said, "So you want to smoke, huh? Go into the house and get me my pipe, and also bring me that big black cigar." He took out his pocket knife and cut up the black cigar and put a piece of it into the pipe.

He said, "You want to smoke? You will smoke, and you *will* inhale." Well, we did, and what an experience. We turned sky-blue pink, yellow, blue, orange and every color of the rainbow! None of us *ever* smoked again!

> **But let all who take refuge in you be glad;**
> **let them ever sing for joy. Spread your protection**
> **over them, that those who love your name**
> **may rejoice in you.**
> **Psalm 5:11**

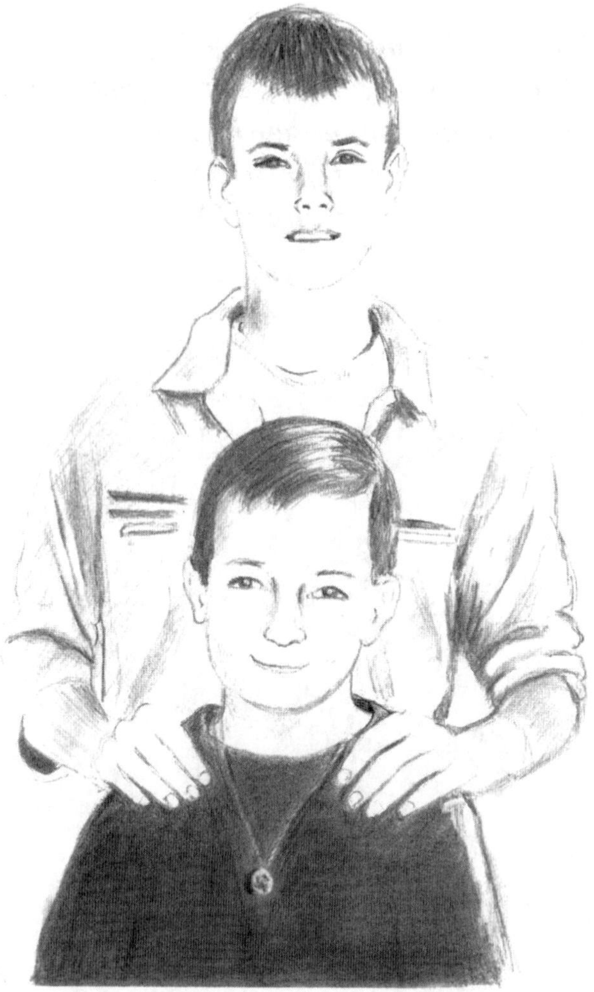

# ALYSSA

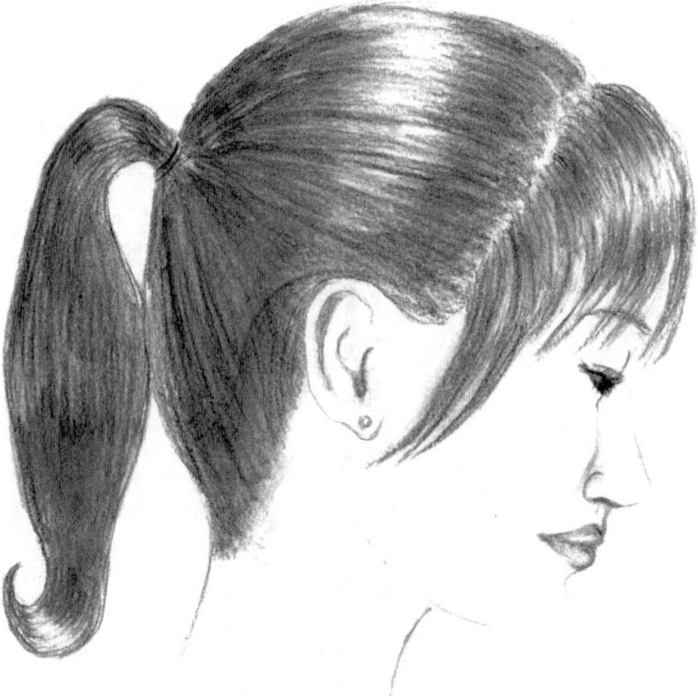

# Alyssa

*Alyssa is a quiet, sweet lady with thick, beautiful hair, and a ready smile for everyone. Her childhood was not an easy one. This is her story as told to me:*

I was born in Maine, to a father who physically abused and molested me. Although he hit me and molested me, I still loved him. Strange isn't it? But, he was all I knew of what a father should be.

My mother was physically abused by my father also, and she drank to avoid her problems. She was a stay-at-home mom who was totally dependent on my father for everything.

My older brother, Bobby, had Cerebral Palsy and was unable to walk. He and I were close. We only had each other.

When I was eleven and Bobby was fourteen, my father contracted Emphysema. He was scheduled to go to the hospital the following week. Dad was very ill and his legs swelled up so that he was unable to walk very well, so I usually helped him do the food shopping. One day Dad drove me to the grocery store. I knew I would have to go in because Dad couldn't walk well enough. On the way to the store, my father told me. "I'm not going to make it to the hospital." Even at the age of eleven, I knew what he meant. After I did the shopping and brought the food to the car, we got home safely. Immediately, Dad started gasping for breath, and he slumped over in the drivers' seat.

I ran upstairs with the grocery bag, screaming, "Mom! Dad collapsed!" She ran downstairs and yelled for help. A nurse who lived next door came quickly to help, but it was too late. Dad was gone.

At his wake, I remember seeing the open, steel-gray casket, and I recall the strong smell of the yellow chrysanthemums. My mother was crying, and people were comforting her. My brother and I were crying off to one side, but I don't remember much else.

It was pouring rain the day of his funeral. As we drove through the gates of the cemetery, a bell was tolling close by. I was afraid.

Days after the funeral, Bobby resumed his life, staying home with my mom. He couldn't go to school because he couldn't walk. In those days they had no provisions for the handicapped. As for me, I continued in junior high school. We were okay financially after my father died because he had been an insurance salesman, so there was a life insurance policy. We lived on that.

Months went by. My mother drank and played morbid music. It was like a scene from an Alfred Hitchcock movie. She couldn't cope with her loss, and she really didn't know how to do basic things. She had been so dependent on my father that she didn't even know how to write a check.

One day, while I was at school, and my mother and Bobby were home alone, my mother collapsed on the floor. My brother, at this time, had lost most of his vision, and he really didn't know what had happened, but he managed to get to the phone. He called a neighbor and she came over. Our neighbor probably thought she was drunk, but not this time. This time it was a stroke.

The ambulance came. The men wrapped her in a chair, and took her down the stairs. She was taken to the hospital, where she stayed for three months. Then they transferred her to another hospital.

I went to live with my aunt, and Bobby went to a sanatorium. Living at my aunt's was the happiest time of my life. My aunt looked a lot like my mom and it was a normal environment there. They had a beautiful garden for me to play in, and cats and dogs to play with. My Grandma lived there. She was 4'9", and bowlegged as could be, but she was always good to me. I loved it there.

After the six months, Mom came out of the hospital and I had to go home with her. I didn't want to. When Mom came home, she had a slight speech impediment, and she walked with a limp. She immediately started drinking again. That's when my uncle came to live with us. He became my mother's trustee in order to help my mother. He helped her all right – helped her right out of her money! After a few months, he wiped out her bank account, left his wife, and took off with another woman.

After that, my mother got on welfare, and that helped us financially. One day, my mother wrote to the Globe Santa and told them about my brother, Bobby, to see if she could get help for him. That's how we met a teacher from the Perkins Institute for the Blind. She read my mom's letter in the newspaper, and came over to help us. She was quite wealthy, and she helped my mother financially. She took wonderful care of Bobby and became his lifeline, as well as ours. This lady lived very frugally herself, but gave liberally to us. She paid two policemen to carry Bobby down the stairs for his outings, and she took care of all of his needs. She was a spinster lady who lived alone and did not have many friends. I didn't know it at the time, but God must have sent her to help us. She helped our family for sixteen years until, at the age of seventy-seven, she died of cancer.

My own personal lifeline was a Sunday school teacher. She was a caring woman who discovered that my mother was an alcoholic. I don't know how she found out about my family, but she started me going to a Baptist Church. It was close enough that I could walk to it. That church sent me to a Christian camp, where I was taught about God. I later accepted Christ, in another Baptist church, at the age of fifteen. It was an awesome experience, with tears of joy. I had been afraid of death my whole life, after seeing my father die, but after accepting Christ, all the fear was gone.

I attended speech class because I had a lisp my whole life. I later learned that a lisp was often caused by molestation. The kids in High School made fun of me because of my lisp and because I didn't have nice clothes. I really hated high school because of that, and when I graduated, I was very glad to get out of there.

I went to nursing school in a work program which paid $25.00 a week, and became a licensed practical nurse. About that time, I met the man who was to become my husband. We married soon after we met. Because my husband was an unbeliever, we couldn't get married at my church, so we got married in the Catholic Church. We had four children together, but it was not a good marriage. Many problems came up because we both had a lot of baggage.

My brother was in the nursing home at this time, and my mother lived alone. One day, she took an overdose of sleeping pills, leaving a note. I was thankful that my aunt found her in time. My mother was unconscious and on a ventilator for five days. I asked the hospital to get her help, but they refused, so my aunt took her in for six years.

When my aunt couldn't take care of Mom any longer, I took her to live in an elderly complex. I had four children and no support, so I couldn't help her any better than that. Less than a year later, I went to visit her at the elderly complex, and was shocked when I found her dead. She had taken pills to end her life.

After my mother died, I was my brother's sole caretaker. I visited him in the nursing home. I read short stories to him, played Yahtzee with him, and played his favorite radio programs for him. Bobby was a good Christian man who loved his Lord. We were bonded together because of our faith. Although crippled, blind, and unable to speak clearly, Bobby said, "I've got lots of friends. There are many people who are worse off than me. My faith in the Lord has kept me going."

Bobby became very ill, and was in a coma for quite a while. We knew that he was dying, but he kept hanging on, not wanting to leave me alone. I didn't know what to do, and his nurse told me to tell Bobby that it was all right for him to leave. I said, "Bobby, fly to Jesus! Fly to Jesus!", and Bobby, who had been in a deep coma, opened his eyes, flapped his arms like a bird flying, and went to his Lord Jesus. He will now have the life he deserves in heaven.

Years went by and the frustrations of marriage broke my husband and me apart. I did try to restore the marriage, but to no avail and so we divorced.

With God's help, I am healing from all the wounds of my past. I can see now that God's hand was on my life from the very beginning. God doesn't take us out of our troubles but gets us through them. He has gotten me through many things, and I am fine today.

There's always a way back. God can take a life of brokenness and bring complete healing. He has done this for me, and he can do it for anyone.

> ***For the Lord your God is God of gods,***
> ***and Lord of lords, the great God, mighty***
> ***and awesome, who shows no partiality and accepts***
> ***no bribes. He defends the cause***
> ***of the fatherless and the widow, and loves***
> ***the alien, giving him food and clothing.***
> ***Deuteronomy 10:17-18***

# PAIGE

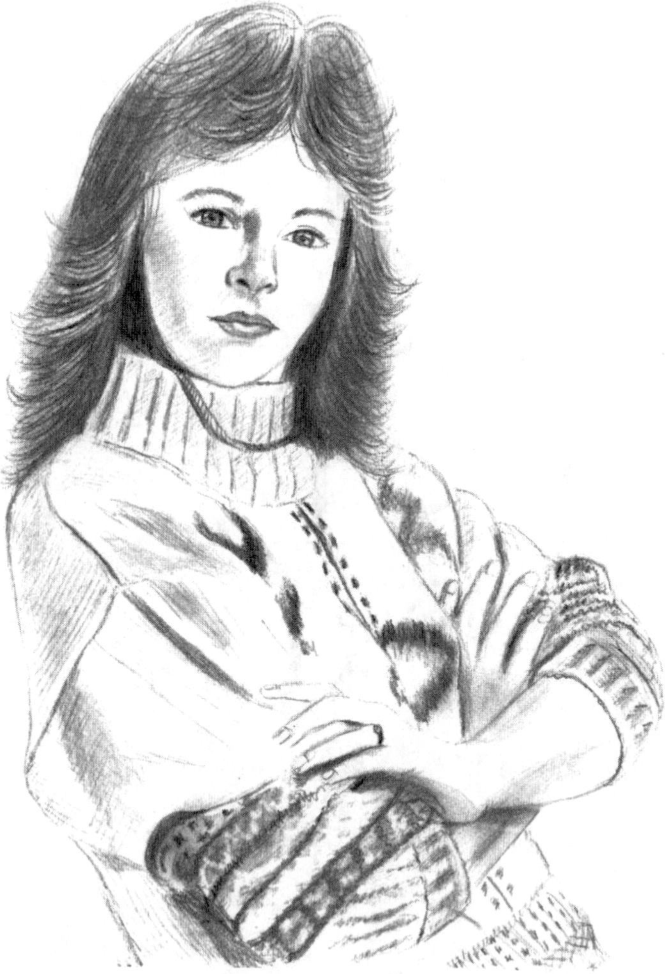

# Paige

*Paige is a sweet lady who is caring, vivacious, and lots of fun to be with. You would never suspect that she had been through such heartache. Here is her story as told to me:*

I went through my early years without knowing my father. They say that you don't miss what you never had, and for a while that was true for me. I don't remember much before the age of five, except for feeling alone. I reminded my mother too much of my father; she hated him, and she reminded me of that at every opportunity. I stayed out of her way as much as possible.

When I was five, my mother remarried. My stepfather did not like me at all. He lied about me often, blaming me for things I did not do, and then my mother would beat me. He often put me out of the house in the cold, rain, and snow. I stayed out until my mother came home from work. My mother and stepfather often fought over me, and it made me feel unloved and worthless. At first I handled it by trying to make others happy. For instance, I would take the blame for things my brother and sister did, just so they would love me. I wanted them to know that I loved them. I had love for everyone, but I never knew what it felt like to receive it.

Things got so bad that when I was twelve or thirteen, I became ill to the point that I couldn't walk properly. I had to be on crutches for a while. I also kept getting into trouble. You see, I figured that if things were going to be bad for me anyway, then I might as well let it be because of something I knowingly and willfully did. I was so mixed up! The things I did served only to hurt me. There was an empty hole inside of me, and it hurt so much! That empty hole deepened and grew darker. The only light I saw that had a spark of love in it was my grandmother. She loved me through it all. I stayed with her for one month and that was wonderful. It didn't last though because my mother didn't want me to get my own way, so she took me back. My grandmother continued praying for me and our family.

As time went on, I heard little facts about my father, and I stored this information, determining that I would try to find him someday. I felt different from the rest of my family like I didn't belong there. Often when I walked down the street I would pass by storefront churches and feel the urge to go inside. I didn't understand why, and I never did go inside, but the urge was strong to go in.

When I was eleven years old, I went to Chicago for the summer to be with my Godmother. I was there for three weeks when my mother called and said she was coming to get me. She said that I had to go home early, but she didn't say why. On the way home, she called me all kinds of names and yelled at me. You see, one of my mother's friends had told her that one of her daughters was pregnant. Of course, my mom assumed it was me. As soon as we got home, she took me to the doctor's office and got me checked out. To my mother's great surprise, the doctor told her I was a virgin. This incident gave me a plan. It stuck in my mind that if I got pregnant, my family would let me go.

When I was fifteen, I ran away at least three times and got myself in a whole lot of trouble. My mother took me to court and I was put on probation. The court gave her total control over my life.

At the age of seventeen, I met a young man who liked me very much. I didn't give him the time of day, but he was always after me. I told him the only way was for us to get married. He was all for it. Now remember, I was on probation so my mother had full control over me. We had to get my mother to agree to the marriage. I knew she wouldn't agree, so I lied and told her I was pregnant, and so she said okay.

When I got married, my new husband got full control over me. I thought this would improve my life, but it was a big mistake. The day after I said I do, I got my first beating from my husband. The beatings continued until I finally left him and went back to my mother's home. My husband was taken to court, and he was given the choice of either going into the service for twenty years, or going to jail for twenty years. He decided to go into the Army. So, I was left on my own, and discovered that I was expecting my first child. All of my old feelings surfaced. I didn't want my child to feel the same way I had felt for so many years, so I went back to my husband. I stayed with him for a while, and became pregnant with my second child. My husband came home for R&R and beat me again almost to the point of death. This scared me enough that, in 1969, I filed for a divorce. The Army wouldn't let me get one, as they protected their soldiers. However, in 1972, three years later, *he* filed for divorce because he wanted to remarry. This was another heartbreak for me – another rejection. So, from 1967 to 1978, I had six children, accepting every kind of hell their fathers dished out to me. I was still looking for love.

In 1999, my best friend, Leslie, and I were talking. I told her all that I had been through in life. I was now physically hurt to the point that I could no longer work. I was homeless and mentally broken. Everything had been taken from me. I had nothing left to lose. I told Leslie that I wished I had met my dad. I said, "I wonder if my life would have been any different if I had had a real dad in my home."

She said, "Let's see if we can find him on the internet."

I laughed nervously, and said, "Okay!"

Sure enough, she found his name in the computer and then found his number in the phone book. I was scared, but Leslie made me call him. A man answered and I said, "I'm looking for a man named James Wilson. Do you know anyone by that name?"

He said, "Yes, that's my name." I asked him if he knew my mother and he said "No."

I asked if he had ever lived in Chicago and he said "My father did." I told him my name and my maiden name. He said, "Wait a minute. Can I call you right back?" I said, "Yes."

A few minutes passed, and then he called back. He asked if I knew his aunt's name, and I said, "Yes, I remember my mother mentioning it."

He said, "I called my aunt, and she said you are my sister, and that they have been looking for you for years!"

I asked him, "Where is our dad?"

My brother replied, "Dad died twenty years ago." My heart sank upon hearing those words.

So that hole in my heart still remained. The good news is that I now have 3 more brothers and many aunts and cousins. So, my family has increased. But, to fill the hole in my heart, I have been given the best Father that a person could ever have. I have accepted Christ as my Savior. Finding the Lord and having a relationship with him has closed the gap in my heart and put a spotlight in that dark place where no one else resided. Now the Lord resides in that place.

I know that my Heavenly Father watched over me all those early years. I should have been dead many times, but God protected me. God knows that we will make mistakes through life, but if we surrender to our Heavenly Father he will slay all our giants.

**Can a mother forget the baby at her breast and have no compassion on the child she has borne? Though she may forget, I will not forget you!**
*Isaiah 49:15*

# GRACE

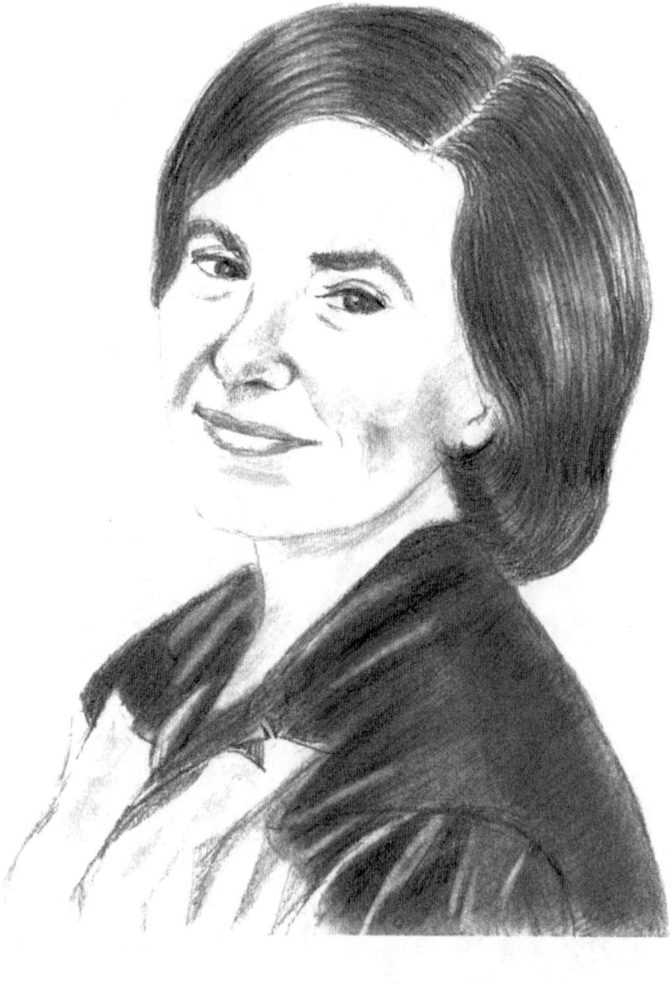

# Grace

*Grace is beautiful, caring, and a wonderful minister of God. It is very evident that she loves the Lord, by the love she shows to her husband, children and everyone she encounters. Here's the story that she tells about her life without a father:*

I am a minister, a wife, and a mother of three. In my ministry, I have been very open about the painful scars that Jesus has healed in my heart. One area, however, which was the closest to my heart, and which has left the most emptiness was the absence of my father. I really did not come to grips with it until after I married and had my three children. God had healed me of abuse and of other things too horrible to share with you, and I will always be grateful to him for that. But when it came to the subject of my father, I pushed it all down and pretended like everything was fine. It seemed to work for a while until I'd see one of my friends with her dad, and then the pain would hit me all over again. For me, the lack of a father was the biggest rejection, and the center of all my insecurities. My father left when I was three years old and I did not see him again until I was seven. He moved far away and would come back occasionally to see us, as if he were Santa Claus. He always brought lots of promises of things he was going to do for us. He never did any of them. At first, he came every year, then every couple of years. When he came he would call me Daddy's Girl, and that is all I had ever wanted.

After that, he moved back, and he promised that things would be different, but I rarely saw him. Dad was still distant and still riddled with guilt each time he saw us. He was an alcoholic and cheated on my mom, so she finally told him to get out. He gladly left to be with his mistress. Later, he married his mistress and had a daughter by her. After that, his world revolved around his new daughter, and I was left wondering what was wrong with me.

Let me tell you a little more about my dad so that you can better understand him. When he was a child, his mother treated him different than his other siblings. He was the reason his mom and dad got married, and I guess she blamed him for that. And so, my father was always trying to gain his mother's favor.

When I was eleven, my mom finally decided to go after him for money. That's when he decided to go back to the big city again. He went out there first and his wife and child were supposed to follow him later. His wife called him and said they weren't coming because she was cheating on him. He had a nervous breakdown because of this. I got word of this the day before I turned thirteen.

Much later, Dad and I started writing letters to each other again, and I regained hope that we would finally have the relationship I had always longed for. But it was not to be. The last time I saw my father was at my grandmother's funeral. I was fifteen. I remember him taking my older brother and me out to eat. He gave us five hundred dollars each that day. It's plain to see that my father felt a lot of guilt because of how he treated us, but he was broken and he *couldn't* be there for us.

Soon after that, my brother got word that our father didn't want anything to do with anyone from the East Coast – especially his children! The pain of hearing that haunted me for a long, long time.

But then, I met someone who changed my life forever. My church taught me that God was my Heavenly Father and that he promised that he would never leave me nor forsake me. I struggled with that concept for a long time. Would God be like my earthly father? My father broke promises and was *never* there when I really needed him. It was difficult for me but I decided to test the waters. So, when I was seventeen, I cried out to God at an altar. I asked him to come into my life and to change me. When I did, I found that God is always true to his word.

These are a few scriptures that helped me through a lot of lonely nights:

> "When my father and mother forsake me, then the Lord will receive me." Psalm 27:10
>
> "When you lie down, you will not be afraid; when you lie down, your sleep will be sweet." Proverbs 3:24
>
> "God is not a man that he should lie, nor a son of man that he should change his mind. Does he speak and not act? Does he promise and not fulfill?" Numbers 23:19

I share this with you to let you know there *is* light at the end of the tunnel. If you give him all your hurts, he will be closer than a brother. Your pain becomes his. In the bible, it says that he has bottled all our tears and has numbered the hairs of our heads. He loves you more than your own parents ever could; he is the Perfect Father. Even good fathers will disappoint you from time to time. God's word is always true. You can run to him and be safe. God has been very good to me. I'm married to a wonderful, Godly man now and have 3 beautiful children.

Just after my second child was born, I wrote my father and told him that I forgave the past. I tried one last time to renew a relationship with him. While doing this, I felt the Lord speak to me. He told me to lay it out there, and then if he didn't respond, to walk away and move on with my life. I've done that. I now have a wonderful family that needs me to be present in the here and now, instead of pining over what *could* have been. You can be sure that God has a destiny for your life. He has a purpose for you to fulfill, something that is bigger than you. Allow God to bring you to a place where you are no longer looking back at past hurts, but instead are looking forward to a life of blessings with God.

***You will go out in joy and be led forth in peace; the mountains and hills will burst forth into song before you, and all the trees of the field will clap their hands. Instead of the thornbush will grow the pine tree, and instead of briars the myrtle will grow. This will be for the Lord's renown, for an everlasting sign, which will not be destroyed.***
***Isaiah 55:12-13***

# DÃVẼ

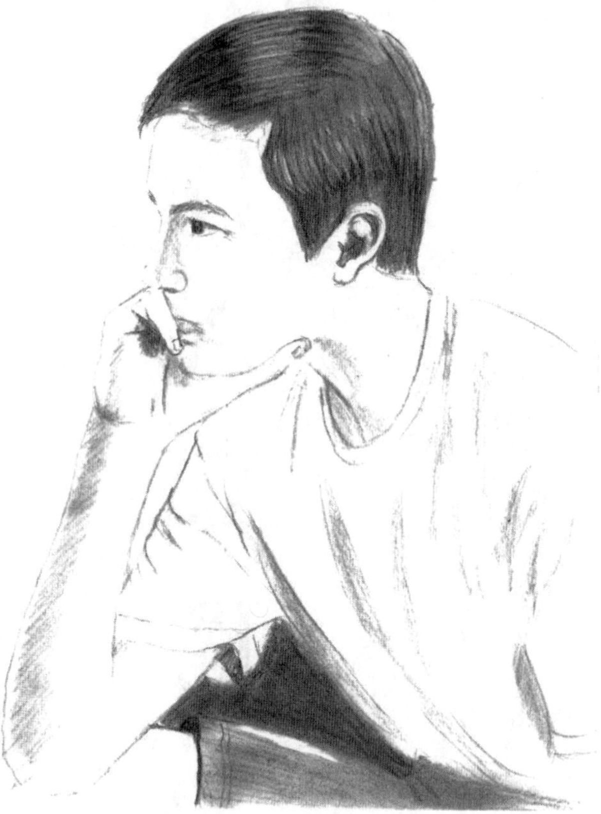

# Dave

*Dave is a man who had a rough beginning, but has totally turned his life around. He is kind and generous, and wants to live to please his Lord. Here's his story:*

My mom and dad had three boys. I was the middle child. My dad worked two or three jobs, and when he came home, he would drink. He never became mean though. I resented the fact that my dad always did stuff with my oldest brother and not with me and my youngest brother. It seemed that he only hung out with me when he needed me to help him do some work. For instance, he took me into the city with him one day so that I could help him. He knew of a place where they were tearing down cobblestone roads. I helped him get the cobblestones and helped him build a stone wall for our yard. Other days we did an ice cream route together. We would sell popsicles and ice cream sandwiches. One year we got chocolate-covered ice cream bars to sell., but we never sold any of those; we ate them all ourselves!

When I was ten or eleven, my father had his first heart attack. Then, one day when I was fifteen, I was helping him paint the bathroom when he grabbed his chest, and slowly started sitting down. He told me to call an ambulance and call a neighbor to go with him to the hospital. I told him I'd go with him and he said no. I think he probably knew he was going to die and he didn't want me to see it.

They contacted my mom and she met him and the neighbor at the hospital. He died there in that hospital. Mom came home and told us and I cried my heart out. My mother took it very hard and withdrew into herself. People comforted my mother, but my brothers and I were left to grieve by ourselves. The doctor said that I was depressed over my father's death, but I would hopefully come out of it. I don't think I did. In high school, I got along with everybody, but I kind of kept to myself.

When I got out of high school I got jobs and that's when I started to learn about life, and how to deal with people and get along with them. I learned to be an electrician at the Quincy Shipyards. In order to fit in with the others, I started drinking with them.

I met a girl, fell in love and got married. We had our first child, a girl, and things were going pretty well. Then we had our second child, a boy. He died when he was only 4 weeks old. When he died, I began to drink heavily. After my son died I became a drunk for ten to twelve years. I just didn't know how to handle his death. People told me to get over it, and move on, but I couldn't. It still bothered me. They didn't understand how it felt. Their words just aggravated me and caused me to drink even more.

After the ten years, my wife took the kids and left me. She had decided that she couldn't take it anymore. So I went to Minnesota to live and there I attended AA meetings. In that program I discovered what they called 'a Higher Power'.

Then, my wife and kids came back to me in Minnesota. She would pray for me at night when I was sleeping, and she would play Christian music for me. I thought to myself, "I don't ever want to become one of these!" By that, I meant I didn't ever want to be a Christian.

After three years in Minnesota, we decided to move back to New England. I attended a Christmas pageant at a Baptist Church. The preacher was a truck driver during the week and, being a truck driver myself, I could relate to him. During the service, I remember the song, "How Great Thou Art" playing, and I was moved so much by it that I accepted Christ as my Savior. I started attending church after that, and living my life for God and serving him.

That's when my life turned around, and I really started living. I learned to trust in God instead of my own heart. Men don't like to hear the word "no", but God sometimes says no to us. He knows best. He loves us, and wants the very best for us. We just need to trust that.

> **Blessed is the man who listens to me,**
> **watching daily at my doors,**
> **waiting at my doorway.**
> **For whoever finds me finds life**
> **and receives favor from the Lord.**
> **Proverbs 8: 34-35**

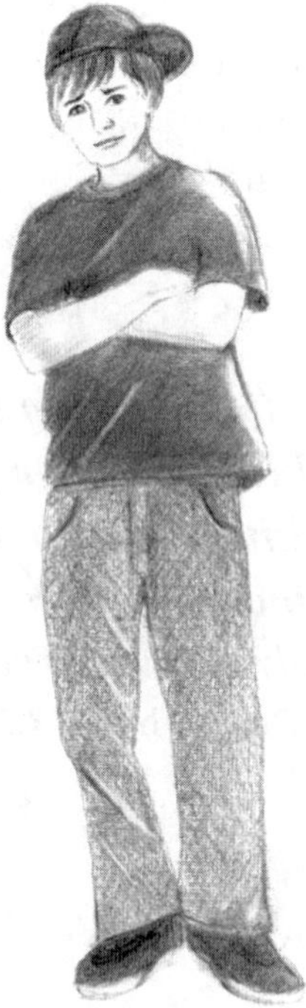

# ELIZABETH

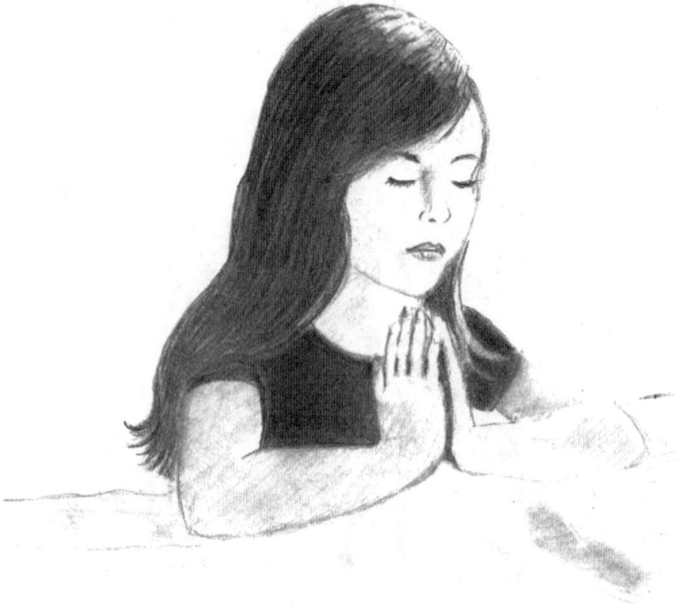

# Elizabeth

*Elizabeth is a very generous and giving woman. She is always ready and willing to help others. This is her story:*

I was the youngest of four children, and was born to a single mother. I never knew my father, and I don't even know his name. No one in the family knows who he is and Mom never talked about him. My mom worked two jobs to support us. During the week she worked in a clothing store and on weekends she worked as a waitress. We had what we needed, but no extras. We were brought up Catholic.

The first five years of my life, were spent mostly with my grandparents. They were wonderful people. My grandfather never raised his voice to us. My grandmother used to tell us stories and pray with us. They were very kind and loving people, and even let us live at their house for two years.

Mom let us go to the Salvation Army Bible School, even though we were Catholic. When I was five, I accepted Christ at that camp. I was taught that God was my Heavenly Father, and I always felt that Jesus was my best friend.

During my teen years, my mom went through menopause and I went through a rebellious period. I couldn't understand her mood swings, and often went to the home of one of my relatives until Mom calmed down. I also went to talk to a priest about what I went through with my mom. He was a good sounding board and he would suggest solutions to my problems. He helped me to grow spiritually.

I felt different when I was a teenager. People thought I was a snob because I didn't get involved in a lot of their activities. But I kept busy babysitting almost every weekend to buy my own clothing and shoes, to help my mom out. She taught us to be responsible and caring to others.

In my early years, I was under the impression that my brother's father was my father. One day, I spoke to him on the phone about it, and he was very nice, but he later sent me a letter saying that he was not my father. He said that he was stationed in the Navy at the time I was conceived. He kindly said that I could still keep in touch with him but I chose not to.

Five or six years later, I spoke to my mom about the letter I received and told her that he was my brother's father but not mine. She got very upset, and I dropped the subject. Mom was ashamed of her past and very embarrassed by it. She had a good relationship with Christ in her later years, and lived alone until the day she died.

When I was seventeen, I met the man I was to marry through a mutual friend. I was attracted to him immediately and liked it that he was a gentleman. We dated for several months and then he asked me to marry him. I prayed to God to let me know if he was the right person for me, and I had a dream that God said he was the right one. After going together for a year and nine months, we got married. About a year after that, I got pregnant with our first baby. We named her Natalie. She was a beautiful baby and very smart.

When I got pregnant with my second baby, I had a dream that he died. I carried him full term, and named him Joshua. When he was four weeks old, he died of acute viral pneumonia. The doctor had checked him that afternoon, and except for a stuffy nose, he was fine. I was told that viral pneumonia strikes an infant up to three years of age and that there's nothing that can be done.

My husband was a non-believer and he started drinking heavily when the baby died. We weren't living as we should, and I realized that and, at the age of twenty-seven, I rededicated my life to the Lord. My husband, on the other hand, was angry with God. It was very hard for me to talk to him about it. So, I turned to God, and he turned away.

We had two more beautiful children – Zachary and Caroline. Then we moved to Washington and I got involved in an Evangelical Baptist church. The children and I started attending that church regularly. I grew closer to the Lord through the good biblical teachings of that church. I prayed that my husband would stop drinking and for God to take the desire for alcohol away from him. In December of 1973, God did just that, and he hasn't had a drink since then.

In 1981, he started going to church with us. He accepted Christ and had an experience that changed his life. Although we've had many trials and problems, God has helped us through them. He has blessed us, and guided us when we lost our way.

Often, when I look in the mirror, I wonder if I look like my father. Did I inherit any health problems from him? I often wonder where he is. Is he still alive? In the past, I'd also often look at men to see if I looked like them. Every once in a while, someone would mistake me for another woman, and I wondered if she was my half-sister. Do I have brothers and sisters that I don't know? These are questions that I wonder about.

Growing up without a dad was difficult and embarrassing because kids would ask about my dad, and I knew nothing about him. God filled that gap for me. I now feel very loved by God and I know that he is with me. I can trust him to watch over me.

> ***And whatever you do, whether in word or deed, do it all in the name of the Lord Jesus, giving thanks to God the Father through him.***
> ***Colossians 3:17***

# IÑEZ

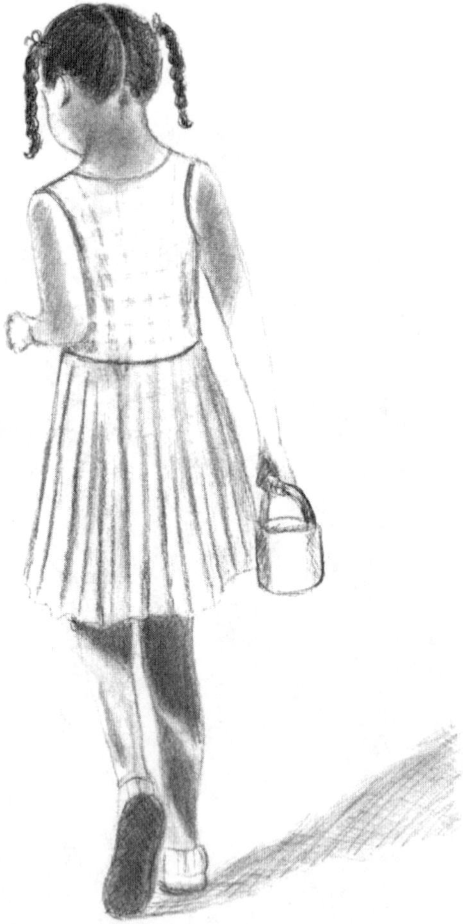

# Inez

*Inez' has spent a lifetime searching for a love that only a father can give. She is a charming woman who loves to read and write. She is also a wonderful storyteller. Here is her story, in her own words:*

I came from a family like so many others, with a long history of what I call "No-Father-Present Syndrome." My mother never knew her father, and her mother never talked about him. I'm assuming my mother's grandmother experienced the same heartache. The cycle continued in my life with my father, as well as with my children.

My dad was born in the British West Indies, on the island of Nassau, Bahamas. My mom was born and raised in Boston. While riding home on a subway in Boston with a friend, she met a very tall and very charming young man. A relationship blossomed, and they married shortly after.

Being newlyweds, they were very happy in the beginning. To seal their love, I was born, and my sister a year after. While we were still very young, my dad left home and went back to the Bahamas and never came back to the States. A light went out in my life that day.

I prayed that he'd miss us enough to come back; but of course that never happened. My Aunt Ruth shared my dad's unspoken words of love for his two daughters in a letter to me once. She also shared with me that he was a troubled soul. She explained that only God knew how he really felt deep down inside about not being with his family.

So now my mom found herself in a position that no young bride would ever care to be in – that of being both mother and father. This was something that she grew up with herself. For years she would struggle financially just to keep a roof over our heads and clothes on our backs; yet she managed to do it with such grace. Anything extra was just that – extra – and that didn't happen very often.

Eventually, mom and dad divorced. She never married again, but she did have more children. I have two sisters, Ivy and Mia, and a brother, Quinn. I also have other siblings on my father's side. My youngest brother's father was a great father figure. I recall his love for music. He played the saxophone very well. He also wrote music as well as lyrics. He taught me to do it too. I remember a song he wrote especially for me. It was awesome!

Besides teaching me music, he helped support my family financially as well as emotionally. However, he too didn't stay around very long. As an adult, I continued to keep in contact with him until his untimely death about 2 years ago. I remember the good times and I hold everything he taught me close to my heart. I miss him dearly.

I went through elementary, middle and, of course, high school all without the presence of a father. Then, when I was 17 years old, I received a message from a family member that would shatter my world even more. My dad had died a tragic death. How would I go on now, knowing that I had no chance of ever seeing him again?

But, you do; you go on because you have to, but it's something that's always with you. I had moved out of my mother's home, probably a year before my dad's death. With my dad gone, and still on my quest of looking for love, I made a few wrong choices along the way.

In my senior year of high school, that all changed. That year, I met and developed a relationship with the most loving and compassionate person I'd ever met. His name was Darnell. Little did I know he would become my high school sweetheart, and eventually my son Tyler's father. History has a funny way of repeating itself. Now I was in a place that my mother once occupied. Darnell and I were faced with the responsibility of raising our beautiful baby boy. Unfortunately, we didn't have a whole lot of experience or maturity to do so without facing a lot of hardships.

We were like most young and inexperienced couples who try to play house without knowing how the mortgage is going to get paid. Eventually, we parted. I painfully convinced myself that it was for the best.

Years later, I did get married, but not to my high school sweetheart. From that marriage, came my second son, Hunter. Darnell married as well. Both of our marriages survived only a few years.

Although our lives took us in different directions, in my heart, Darnell was still my guy! I remained single. Darnell remained single as well, vowing never to marry again unless it was to his first love. I began to wonder, would the road that led us to each other so many years ago as teenagers, lead us back into each other's arms as adults?

God obviously heard both of our prayers, because our love survived, and over 30 years later, we're looking forward to planning our wedding.

Unfortunately, my dad never learned how to be a father. As the saying goes, "When you know better, you do better." My prayer is that my children will do better.

**The Lord is close to the brokenhearted,**
**and saves those who are crushed in spirit.**
**Psalm 34:18**

# MATT

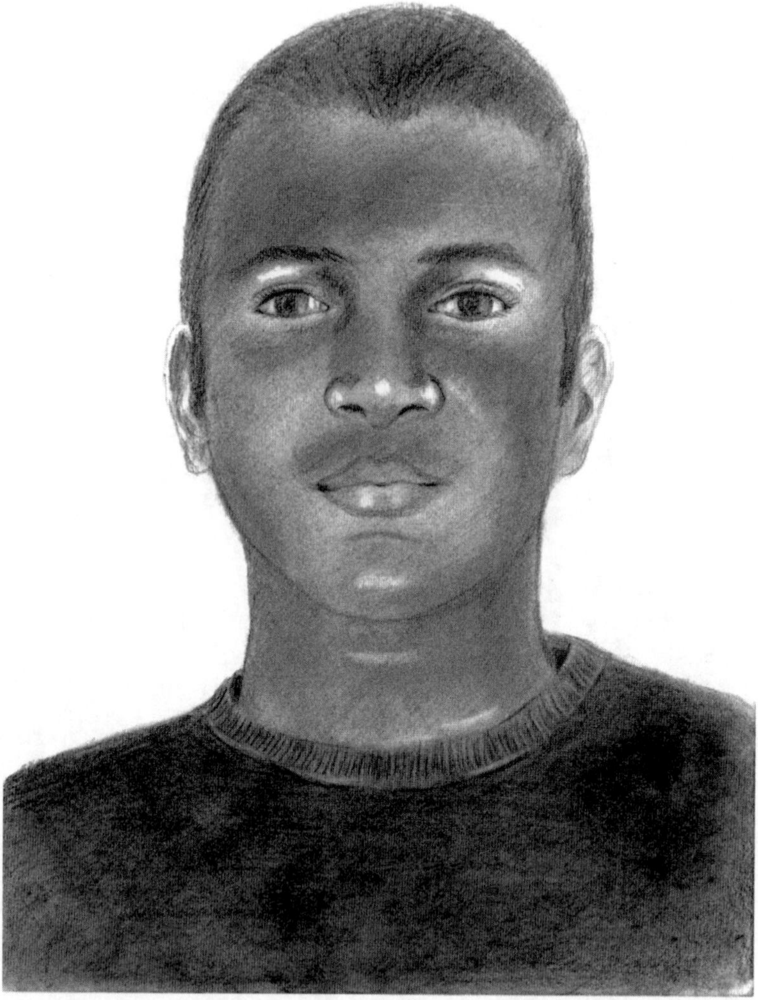

# Matt

*Matt is a well-spoken, polite, young man who speaks English fluently although he was not born in this country. Here is his story, in his own words:*

My name is Mathias, but everyone calls me Matt. I was born in Fiji and was brought up Hindu. When I was eight or nine years old, my family broke up. I started going to a Salvation Army Church where I attended a children's program. There was an altar call given and it really moved me. I remember getting down on my knees, putting my head down and folding my hands. A man came over to me, prayed for me, and I accepted Christ as my Savior. After accepting Christ, I prayed and asked God to bring my family back together again. A few months later, my family did get back together and I felt that God had answered my prayer and was calling me to come serve Him. Coming from a Hindu background, it is a big no-no to leave family tradition and religious views. Becoming a Christian would be very difficult, but I didn't know that. One day, Mom overheard me singing Christian songs, and she told me, "Don't let your father hear you singing Christian songs. He's going to get really mad!" I got scared and listened to my mom, and forgot about Christianity.

When I was thirteen, my parents got divorced. I believed it was my mom's fault and I hated her for that. She took my two little brothers, got a job, and went to live with her mother. I went to live with my father's parents. My dad left all of us and went to live in Australia.

I passed my exams in eighth grade with good marks and made it into high school. One day, my uncle bought me a video game, so my six-year-old brother and my nine-year-old brother came over and we played the game. They were supposed to be back to my grandmother's at a certain time, but they got involved in the game and went back a half hour late. So when they went back home, my grandmother was very angry. She said, "You love your other grandparents more than me, so why don't you go live with them!" She kicked them out and my brothers came back to my father's parents' home. They were crying inconsolably. My dad's family took them in, and we lived there very happily together.

Years passed and I graduated from high school when I was eighteen, and I got my visa to go to Australia. There, I reunited with my dad.

When I was nineteen, I started playing Rugby with a friend whose father was a pastor. My friend helped me to recommit my life to the Lord. I remember that it happened in a van in Australia. This time I did it for good – absolutely no turning back. I totally left my Hindu religion behind. When I told my father what I had done, he had no problem with that.

At the age of twenty-one, I went back to Fiji. When one of my relatives heard that I had accepted Christ, he gave me a hard time. He saw me as a weak person for becoming a Christian. When I applied for my Visa to go back to Australia, it didn't go through and so he said, "Where's your God now?" I told him that my God would see me through.

Shortly after that, I won a Green Card Lottery and got a green card to come to America! I shouted, "Well, here is my God! He's seen me through!"

And that's how I came here to America. Coming to this country by myself was a lonely prospect, but I know God was with me through it all. I'm twenty-nine now and have gone to school for Information Technology and will soon get my American Citizenship. My mom hasn't been part of my life for seventeen years. My father hasn't been in my life physically since he's been overseas, but he's been there for me whenever I've needed help. He's often helped me out financially when I needed it. I have forgiven my mom and my dad. Life's been difficult, but God is a father to the fatherless and he kept revealing himself to me. I've been in America for six years now and I have a good job, my own apartment, and a wonderful fiancée. I can do all things through Christ which strengthens me. God has had his hand on me all of my life. Glory be to God!

> ***Trust in the Lord with all your heart***
> ***And lean not on your own understanding;***
> ***In all your ways acknowledge him,***
> ***And he will direct your path.***
> ***Proverbs 3: 5-6***

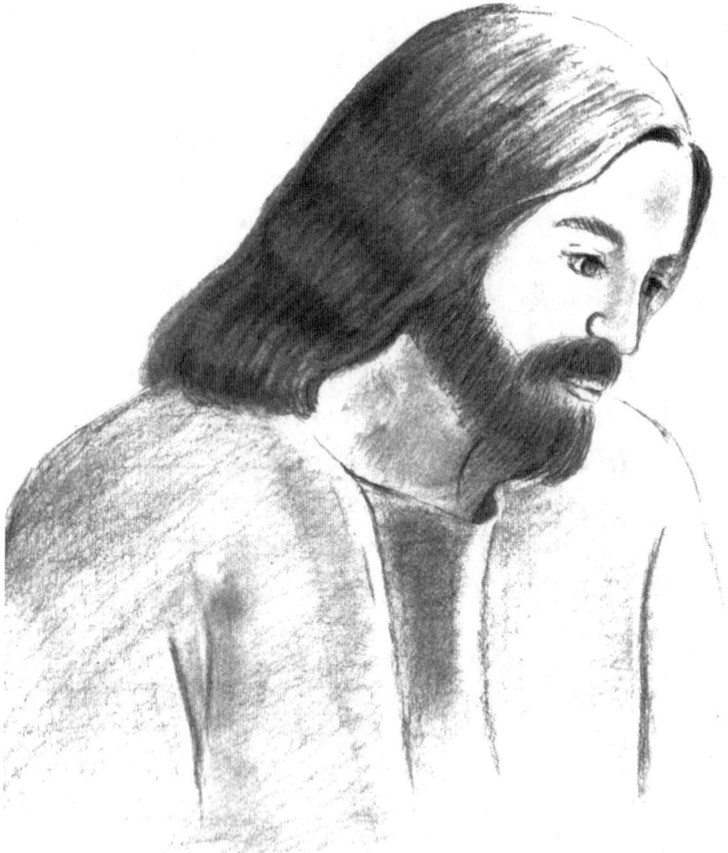

# ARMIÑDA

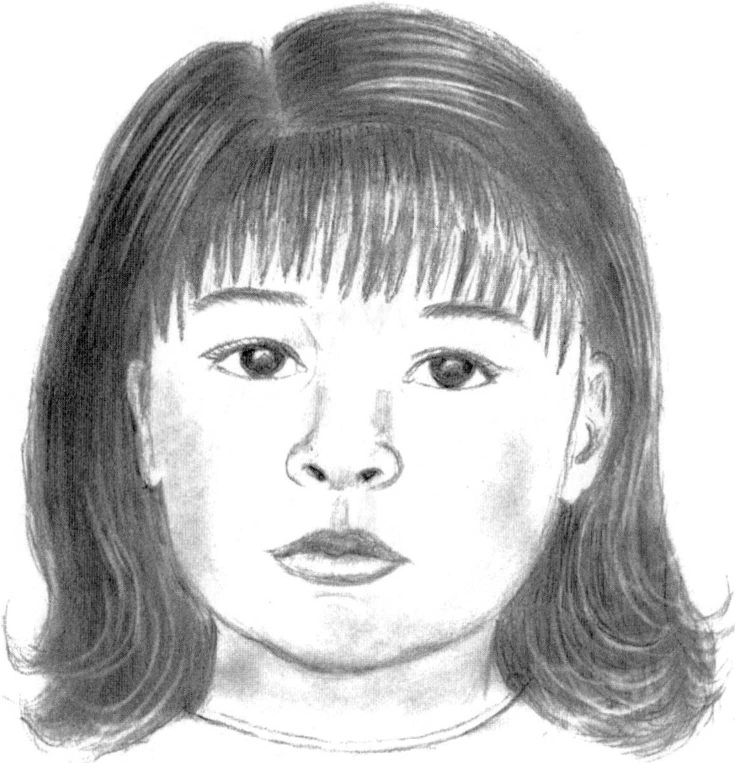

# Arminda

*Arminda is a quiet, unassuming woman who loved her father very much. She cried many tears as she told me her story:*

I was the oldest of four children – three girls and one boy. My mom and dad were born on the island of Brava, Cape Verde Islands. My father traveled back and forth to the United States to work as a chef in a restaurant in the northeast. He brought my mother to the U.S. and that's how my sister and I happened to be born in the U.S. instead of Cape Verde.

Father wanted my mother, my sister, and me to stay in the U.S. with him. We did stay for five years. Then, after receiving a message that his parents were ill, my father, mother, baby sister and I returned to Cape Verde. My father stayed there with us for two years. He built us a beautiful home, and then returned to work in the U.S. Although our father was away from us more than he was with us, he wrote to us, and sent us clothes, shoes, and all kinds of goodies. He always thought of us. He wrote my mother and asked her to bring the children and come to him in the U.S. He said he needed us there. Life wasn't good without us. But, my mother had one of the most beautiful houses in Brava and she wasn't about to leave it, so she refused. She said she'd come for a visit, but he told her to sell the house and come. She refused to do it. He told her that she couldn't come to him unless she sold the house. And so we stayed there. We children were not happy about my mother's decision, but we could not persuade her to leave her house.

So, our father continued to visit us every few years. Another girl was born, and so there were three of us girls. Being the oldest, I knew our father best. He was always loving and kind to me. He told my mother that I had his temperament, and didn't need spanking. He said that I had a quiet spirit and would obey with just a word. This was true. My mother listened to him, and although she did occasionally spank the other children, I was never spanked. This was one way that my father showed his love for me. He looked after me even when he wasn't there.

Whenever we got word that my father was coming, there was great excitement! My sisters hardly knew him, as they were too little to remember him, but they picked up on my excitement and grew excited too. When he came, he would devote his time to our family. He would help my mother, and play games with us children. He was a great storyteller and would tell us stories about animals that could talk. We loved hearing them. He always brought presents to us, as well as to friends and family. He was a very generous man who loved people, and everyone loved him. He always had to go back to the U.S to work though, and he never did persuade my mother to join him there. And so, he returned to the U.S. again. After he left, my little brother was born.

When I was fourteen, I got up one morning, and my mother told me, "Arminda, I had a dream about your father last night. Perhaps he's on his way to see us. In my dream he had on a white shirt, and he had a button missing and had a safety pin holding the shirt together."

I said, "Oh, Mama, I hope that the dream means that he's coming! Wouldn't that be wonderful?" And so, we had breakfast, and talked about my father's arrival, and how awesome it would be.

Later that afternoon, my uncle and my mother's cousin knocked at our door. My mother went to open it. They stood on the doorstep, and their faces said it all. My mother started crying. She kept repeating, "Oh Jose! Oh, Jose! Oh, my Jose!", and that's how we found out our father had died. My uncle had received a telegram from a relative in the U.S. My father had developed a blood clot in his leg from all those years of standing in his job as a chef. Today, such a blood clot would easily be repaired, but in those days, they didn't have the technology, and so it killed him.

It saddened us that we couldn't attend the funeral that they had for him in the United States, but we were grateful that we had family there who would take care of it for us. As for us, we had a memorial service for him at our home in Brava, and many people attended. He was so loved! My brother was only four years old when our father died. He had never even met his father.

For three years we all wore black to show our grief. That was the custom in those days. My mother worked hard and she provided for us. She was a very strong woman and brought us up right. We respected her, knowing she had a tough job with the four of us, and so we helped her all we could. My father thought of us even in death. We received a check every month even after he had died. That helped us out financially.

Years later, I got married and came to the U.S. with my husband and baby girl. We worked hard and bought a house, then sent for my mother, two sisters and brother. It was a three-family home and so there was enough room for all of us. We lived in two of the apartments, and rented out the third. Everyone in the family got a job and helped to support the family. My mother eventually sold her house in Brava. I've seen pictures of it as it looks now. It's still one of the most beautiful old homes there. I guess my mother finally realized that people are more important than things.

I still miss my father. When I think about it; I guess I hardly knew him. But I loved him a lot, regardless. Someday, I hope to see him again in heaven, and then we'll be together forever – me and my dad.

> *Have mercy on me, O God, have mercy on me,*
> *for in you my soul takes refuge.*
> *I will take refuge in the shadow of your wings*
> *until the disaster has passed.*
> **Psalm 57:1**

# JULIE

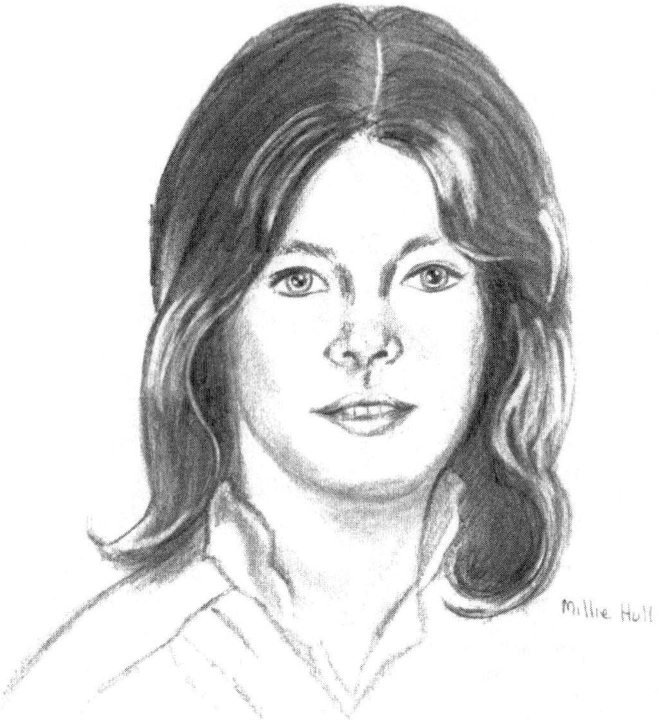
Millie Hull

# Julie

*Julie is a pretty lady, who is very petite, and athletic-looking. She is fun to be around, and wants to help others by telling her story.* Here's what she told me:

I was the youngest of three children. My mom was forty years old when she had me. My sister was sixteen and my brother was fourteen when I was born, so I guess I was quite a surprise to them.

One winter, when I was two years old, my brother was babysitting me while my father was outside shoveling. When my father came inside from shoveling, he sat down at the kitchen table and grabbed at his chest and slumped over. It was a heart attack! My brother tried to help him, but it was too late. I don't know where my mother was at the time of my father's death. I was two, and in my crib at the time, so I know all of this only because my brother and sister told me when I grew older. They also said that my mother and father never got along. They were either arguing, or not speaking to each other. My brother never had any kind of relationship with our father. My sister had a little bit, as she was the oldest, but not much.

After my father died, my mother started dating and going to Portuguese clubs. When she went out, she would leave me here and there with people. Every time she left me somewhere, I would get sick. It was probably separation anxiety, but I don't really know. She sometimes left me with people that I didn't even know, and I would get a sick feeling in my stomach and throw up. Even if my sister and brother babysat me, I still got sick. I'd get nervous and all worked up. When I was ten, eleven, twelve and thirteen, my mother would leave me places so she could go out to the clubs, but she would never let me sleep over for the entire night. She always came to get me at two o'clock in the morning so that she didn't have to go home and sleep by herself. She had anxiety problems, and it seems like I have it too now.

I did well in school, but I absolutely hated it. And then, on holidays, when it's supposed to be so much fun and everyone wants to be home from school, I was miserable. Holidays were just terrible! My mother was always complaining about all the cooking she had to do. She was never happy. She only seemed happy when she was going out.

When I went to high school, I stopped doing well in school because I started smoking pot and taking pills. I did it just because it was there, and my friends did it. I had no direction whatsoever. There was no one there to notice or tell me it was wrong. I left home when I was eighteen, and stayed with my friend's family for a while until I got my own apartment.

After high school, I went to Johnson and Wales College. I didn't want to because I was a singer and wanted to study music, but my sister said I should take a Secretarial Business Course, so I did. After that, I worked for a while as a bank teller. I quit that job and then got office jobs. I would get a job and quit, and then get another one and quit that. I didn't have any direction, and I blame myself for that. I hated doing secretarial work so I went into sales. I liked it, but I didn't like the instability of commissions. I stayed in sales for a while, selling furniture. It was a very good job. We traveled to different factories and that was fun. We created in-depth information which persuaded people to buy the furniture. But that job eventually slowed down. I also wanted to get out of working for commissions, so I went to work as a secretary for a dentist. I've worked there for 11 years now. I don't love it, but it's what I have to do.

A year after I bought my condo, I met my husband. He was in the restaurant business. I married him a year later. We were happy at first, but then three years later, something happened to change all that. He didn't come home one night until four o'clock in the morning, and so I went looking for him. I found his car parked in front of the house of a girl I knew. That's how I found out he was cheating on me. So, I divorced him.

After that, I went out with a guy that I met in college. He got me into weight lifting and I did that for one and a half years, but that didn't work out because of his son and his ex-wife. Then I joined a gym and met someone there that taught Karate. We started walking and exercising together. We got into Hybrid Road Biking, and that keeps us busy on the weekends. I had gotten caught in the trap of working, eating and sleeping, and I never did anything enjoyable. But, now that's changed, and I have some enjoyment in my life. I don't do drugs, I eat right, exercise, try to do the right thing, and ask for guidance daily. I'm happier now than I've ever been. For once, I'm doing what I want to do. Twice a year, I take a vacation, and take time out for fun, instead of working all the time. Yes, things have definitely turned around for me.

When a person doesn't have a father growing up, they're always searching for a security blanket, a shoulder to cry on, a kiss goodnight, a hug, reassurance, unconditional love, and someone to count on. I haven't quite found that yet, but someday, I know I will.

***Those who sow in tears will reap with songs of joy. He who goes out weeping, carrying seed to sow, will return with songs of joy carrying sheaves with him.***
***Psalm 126: 5-6***

# RICARDO

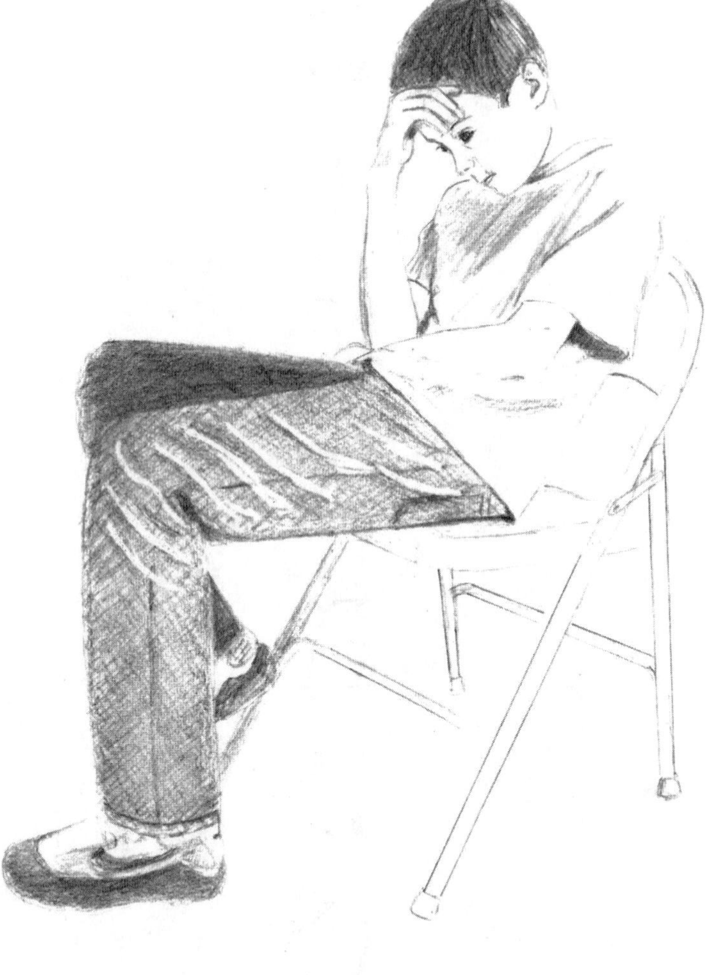

# Ricardo

*I have never met Ricardo, since I only spoke to him on the phone, but I found him to be charming and sincere. He told me his story in order to help others who have lost their fathers in war:*

My father's family is from Central America and are of Spanish descent. He met my American mother at a dance in Boston and married her. They had two children – my sister, who was born in Miami, and me. I was born in El Salvador.

I was very close to my father. He was an amazing man, and everyone loved him. My father had a different philosophy of life. He cared so much about others that he even gave away land to the needy. He loved my mother, sister, and me very much.

When I was little, the Cold War was going on in Central America, and Communist Guerillas had taken over Nicaragua. They wanted to take over El Salvador also. It was a terrible time. To keep us safe, my father sent my mother, my sister and me to the United States. He stayed in El Salvador in order to work and support us. The habit of the Communist Guerillas was to kidnap members of families, and then hold them hostage. They usually wanted a hefty ransom. This was how they got their money to buy arms for the war. The government wanted to keep the workers from going off to war, so they confiscated people's land, and allowed the poor workers to farm it.

I came from a middle-classed family. We owned some land and cattle, but that was before the Communist Guerillas came along. In six months, they took away everything! I remember that my mother, sister and I were living near Boston at the time. I was nine years old, and my mother had planned to send me to camp in Texas. Just before I was to leave, we got word that my father had been kidnapped in El Salvador. My mother was distraught. The Communist Guerillas wanted a lot of money to return my father to us. But, since they had taken away our land and cattle, there was nothing to sell in order to get the money for them. We had no recourse of action.

My mother made the difficult decision to send me to camp anyway, and so I went, knowing that my father had been kidnapped. I was 9 years old, alone, and had no one to talk to about my problems. It was a very bad time for me. I hated camp. The only part of camp that I liked was the swimming. I was so worried about my father that I couldn't begin to have a good time.

The last night of the camp, just before I was to go home, something strange occurred. They had a big campfire, doused a huge cross with gasoline, and tried to set it on fire. For some reason, it did not light. I was so glad that it didn't. To this day, I don't understand what that was about. Were they part of the Ku Klux Klan? I just don't know. What I'm sure of, is that my mother didn't know about this. She was a strong Catholic and wouldn't have sent me if she knew about that.

The next day, I waited for my mother to pick me up to take me home. I waited all day and she never came. It was very stressful for me – first my father was kidnapped, and now my mother doesn't come to pick me up! Some friends from San Antonio finally came to get me. I was told that there had been an emergency that my mother had to take care of. I didn't know what was wrong and was left to wonder about it.

Days later, my mother returned and told my sister and me that my father was dead. That's when my childhood came to an end and my heart was broken. That's when I was told that my beloved father had been killed by the Communist Guerillas.

My mother had been called and told that my father's body was found in a Volkswagen bus. They told her where the body was and said she should come and pick it up. So this was how my mother found out that my father was dead. Can you imagine the horror of receiving that phone call? But she had to be strong, because in that country, bodies had to be buried within twenty-four hours. She immediately left for El Salvador to bury him. My sister and I were left behind to grieve our father's death.

When my mother returned, we tried to get our lives back to normal, but normal wasn't normal anymore. She took what we had and we moved in with her parents. She got a job doing artwork and with her parents help, we got by. I went to elementary school and then high school.

My mother eventually remarried. He was a widower, a very good man and a good father to us. He taught me to work and to get dirty – something I had never learned how to do. The good work ethics I have today are thanks to my stepfather. He had two sons, and my two stepbrothers and I got along well. They were five years and three years older than me. My stepfather and my mother had a good marriage and are still together today.

I went to college and started my own business. I got married at the age of 22, and we had two daughters. My marriage lasted fifteen years, and then we got divorced.

One day, when I was in my thirties, an acquaintance contacted me and said, "All those people who killed your father have been taken care of. There's still one person alive though, and if you want, we can take care of him for you." This may sound like something out of a movie to you, but this is the way things were done in El Salvador in those times of war.

I told him that I didn't want to do it. I knew it would damage my soul, wouldn't bring my father back, and my beloved father wouldn't have wanted me to do such a thing. He was such a good man. I'll let God take care of those who killed him.

And so, I am more fortunate than most. Some have had no father, and I have been blessed with two very good fathers. I pray that I will be a good father to my own two daughters.

**May our Lord Jesus Christ himself and God our Father, who loved us and by his grace gave us eternal encouragement and good hope, encourage your hearts and strengthen you in every good deed and word.**
**2 Thessalonians 2:16**

# DAÑIEL

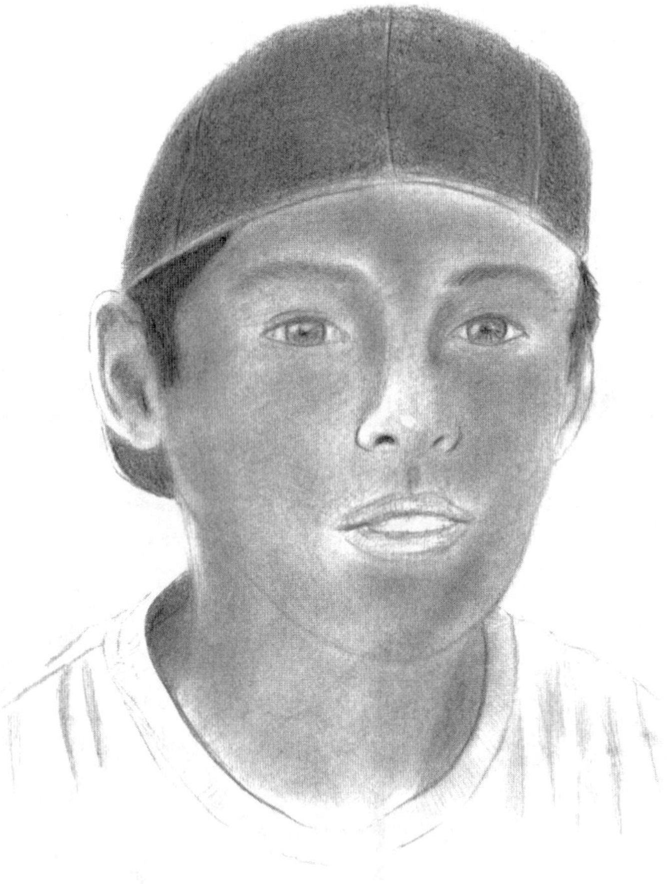

# Daniel

*I met Daniel at Friend Day at my church. Daniel is a 22 year old who is friendly, charming, well-spoken and intelligent. Most people like him on sight. He looked clean and neat and no one would have suspected that he was homeless.*

Friend Day is an outdoor event that we have every year where members invite a friend to attend. This year it included a cookout with lots of food, face painting, a jumpy for the kids, games, and an illustrated message with an altar call. When I first saw Daniel, he was sitting in a fold-up chair, leaning forward on the edge of his seat. Unbeknownst to me, a young girl at our church had met him at the town library and invited him to Friend Day. I kept watching him because, unlike some of the other visitors, he seemed very interested in my pastor's words. When the pastor gave the invitation to come forward to accept Christ, I prayed that he would go up. Several people did go up and I was happy to see that Daniel was one of them.

A little later, while I was in the food line, Daniel came up and stood behind me. I asked him if he'd enjoyed the message and he told me that the message really spoke to him. He told me that he went up and asked for prayer to get closer to the Lord. I asked him if he had accepted Christ as his Savior and he said that he had done so at his mother's church, but that he wasn't sure that he understood it. I asked him if he really meant it when he accepted Christ, and he told me that he probably was just trying to impress his mother. So we talked some more and I told him about Adam and Eve and how sin entered the world through their actions. We talked about the Ten Commandments and how impossible it is for us to obey them. I explained that God sent his Son, Jesus, to die for us to save us from our sins. When I asked him if he had a dad, he said, "No." So I told him that God could become his dad and that

God was the greatest dad ever! I could see that the Holy Spirit was working on his heart. By the time we got to the front of the food line, Daniel had decided to accept Christ as his Savior. I asked him if he really meant it this time and he said, "Yes. I'm not trying to impress you because I don't even know you." So, after we ate our meal, we went inside to a quiet place and he accepted Christ. I believe that Daniel had a heartfelt experience with God that day. He continued to come to church after that and we became friends. One day I asked him if he wanted to be in my book and he said, "I'd love to!" And so, this is Daniel's story:

I was born when my mom was only seventeen years old. She was addicted to drugs and was unable to take care of me. My dad left when I was born, so I was placed with my aunt. I stayed with her for three years, but then my aunt was unable to continue taking care of me. Foster care placed me with a Spanish lady. She only spoke Spanish, which was fine because that's all I spoke at the time. She adopted me and I remained with her until I was fifteen.

Then I started getting in trouble at school. I went from foster home to foster home, and then to a juvenile facility. From there I was moved to a secure detention facility. I got into a few incidents there and was put in lockdown. From there I was discharged into a residential facility in Massachusetts where things got better for me. There were good counselors there who got me to open up to them. I did well until some new people came into the facility. There were some gang incidents and I got in the middle of that. I really wanted to change, but I didn't know how. I was only seventeen at that time.

When I turned eighteen, I wanted to sign myself out of the residential facility. The counselors encouraged me to stay, but I didn't listen. Instead, I went into a subsidized housing program. I was happy there, but I didn't really know what I was doing. I thought being eighteen was great, but all of a sudden I had all this crazy freedom; it was one big party! It started with weed, alcohol, and girls. I used my apartment to party, but my landlord didn't like that. On my nineteenth birthday, on New Year's Eve, I got kicked out of my apartment. I was told that I had until the 31st to get out.

From there I moved to Massachusetts and then to Pennsylvania. The girlfriend I had at the time told me, "You need mending. You should go find your mom." I thought that was a good idea, so I looked for her on the computer. I finally found her on MySpace. I was so excited! I called her and we talked for hours on the phone. She told me she's changed. She's not on drugs anymore. She's become a Christian; she's going to college and she even sings in church! She wanted to see me. Since I had lost my apartment and my job, she bought me a plane ticket to go see her.

When I met my mom, she gave me a hug and she didn't want to let me go. It was a wonderful day for me! I stayed with her and her husband. He tried hard to be nice to me, but I'd never had a father figure in my life before and so I could not get along with him. They were good to me though. They paid for me to get my GED, and bought me furniture for my room.

My mom and her husband were at work all day. I had no car and no way to support myself. So I stayed inside all day and got depressed. My mom thought that I missed New York so she bought me a plane ticket to go back there. I didn't really want to get back to New York, but I figured that I had outstayed my welcome, so I left. It was hard leaving my mom. She was so good to me.

I had a friend in Boston, so I went there. I stayed in my friend's dorm room for a week. I felt free but there were more problems so I chose to leave. From there I went back to New

York again. I stayed with my uncle, and found a job the first week–flipping burgers at a restaurant. I worked there for three months and I bought new clothes and a new phone. But I didn't like the rules and so I lost my job. My uncle was not happy about that, and he also thought I was a bad influence on his children. I probably was. He gave me a week to leave, so I packed up and left.

I moved into a youth shelter. This gave me a job and housing and that was good. But then another relative gave me a call and asked me to move in with him. When I did, I started doing some destructive behaviors. I knew it wasn't good for me to be there. So, when a guy offered to take me to Massachusetts, I accepted. That's how I got to meet the girl at the library who invited me to her church. When I saw her, I thought she was cute, but she only talked about her studies and her church. I was interested because she was different. She invited me to Friend Day at her church so I went. It was a big cookout, with lots of activities. The people were friendly and the bible message touched me like never before. I accepted Christ as my Savior that day. It was a real experience for me. I called my mom and told her what I did. She was so happy!

I'm leaving soon to go to Florida to see her. She's going to get me into a Christian rehab facility to help me get off of my destructive behaviors.

I really do want to change my life and I believe that Christ can help me do it. I want God to be my Father from now on. I pray that this will be a new beginning for me!

> *The Lord will fulfill his purpose for me;*
> *Your love, O Lord, endures forever –*
> *do not abandon the works of your hands.*
> **Psalm 138:8**

# GLORIÃ

# Gloria

*Gloria is a pretty young woman who loves the Lord with all of her heart. Her face glows with the light of God's love. This is her story:*

I never knew my dad. My mom left him before I was born. He was an alcoholic and it was a very bad situation for my mom. After she left him, my mom started dating a policeman. I was still a baby at that time. He was like a dad to me, and he was there any time I needed anything. He didn't live with us, so I always knew he wasn't my real father. When I was thirteen, my mom broke up with him. She later got married to another man who became my stepfather. He was very good to me. He provided for me and helped me out when I was in a jam. I grew to love him very much.

When I was thirteen, my Godmother came in contact with my real father, and he started asking about me. She said that she'd check with me and my mother to see if it was all right for him to see me. In order to do this, she arranged to have me sleep over her house, and she had him over as a guest. She introduced me to him, not as my father, but as a friend. He was there for the whole day. I liked him, and thought that he was a nice guy. He was funny and polite, but I did notice that he drank too much. After he spent the day with us, he went home and came back the next day. While he was in the kitchen, my Godmother asked me if I'd like to meet my real father. I said, "Okay, yes!" She asked me to call my mother to make sure it was alright.

When I asked my mother if it was all right for me to see my father, she said, "I don't care."

So my Godmother walked me into the kitchen and she pointed to my real father and said, "*That* is your father."

I really looked at him then, and realized that I looked exactly like him. I was very confused. He didn't seem like a bad man, yet all my life, I was told that he *was* bad. I was so happy and excited that I couldn't sleep for a whole week afterwards. All the pieces of the puzzle came together in that one sentence, "*That* is your father."

After that day, I didn't keep in contact with my dad regularly. My mom still kept telling me bad things about him and I believed her. My dad couldn't call me at home because my mom wouldn't allow it, and so we lost contact with each other.

And so then, when I was in my mid-twenties, my dad moved to Florida. I got married and started working a state job. My Aunt Jean, who was my dad's sister, started working in the same state program. I didn't even know that she existed, and yet she lived in the same town as I did. By total coincidence, she was sent to work with me. When I was introduced to her for the first time, she recognized me. "Oh my goodness!" she said. "You're my niece!"

She called up her other sister in Florida and told her about me. Her sister expressed a strong interest in talking to me, so my Aunt Jean gave me her sister's phone number. She asked me to call her sister and talk to her. I thought to myself, "I don't want to talk to her!" Eventually though, I did call my aunt in Florida and we became good friends. She told me a lot of good things about my dad. She told me that she was a Christian, and that my father had become one too. But that fact didn't make a real impression on me because I wasn't a Christian. She told me that he'd stopped drinking, that he had a really good job, and that he asked about me often. But the things my mother had told me about him continued ringing in my ears.

At this time in my life, I started having lots of problems. When my husband and I had our first child, a daughter, she was diagnosed with Autism. My husband and I loved her so much, and this diagnosis caused problems in our marriage. I was very unhappy and didn't know what to do, and so I started calling my dad. He would call me back and we'd talk. After he got my phone number, he started calling me regularly. I realized that he wasn't the drunk that I was told about and that he was a genuine person. He started to talk to me about the Lord and I was receptive to it. He was compassionate and he wasn't at all judgmental. My father got me in touch with a relative here who was a Christian and we talked for a week about the Lord. She invited me to her church and I went. I thought everyone was really nice there. The music was awesome and I was so moved by it that I started crying. The sermon was about healing and I needed a healing in my spirit. After the sermon, there was an altar call for healing and prayer and I went up. I felt better afterwards. When the service was over I went downstairs and my relative and her friends talked to me some more about the Lord and that's when I decided to accept Christ. Afterward, I felt like I was on cloud nine! It was an awesome experience!

After I accepted Christ, the healing started between my dad and me. A Christian friend said to me, "You've never forgiven your dad, have you?" I was surprised that she asked me that because she didn't even know my story. I didn't understand how she knew it, but I realized that I did need to forgive him. I prayed with my friend on the phone and confessed to God all of my unforgiveness against my dad. I felt free after I forgave him. It was like a great load was lifted off of me.

And, now, my dad and I are very close. I don't even identify him with the father who wasn't there for me. He's there for me now, and I've grown to love him.

Now, I've gone from having no father at all, to having a stepfather, my real father, and my Heavenly Father. Who could ask for more?

> ***Praise be to the Lord, for he has heard my cry for mercy. The Lord is my strength and my shield; my heart trusts in him, and I am helped. My heart leaps for joy and I will give thanks to him in song.***
> ***Psalm 28:6-7***

# Why Does God Let Bad Things Happen To Us?

I was being interviewed by a newspaper reporter about my book, and he asked me some very important questions. He asked, "If God is so good, why does he let bad things happen?" He went on to tell me that his brother died when he was just a little boy. "Why did God let that happen if he's such a great God?" he said.

Well, I tried to answer those questions, but looking back, I don't think I did such a great job of it. I started thinking though, that it would be important to answer those questions in this book. Why, if God loves us so much, does he let bad things happen to us? He's all-powerful, so he can stop anything from happening, right? So, why doesn't he?

These are very difficult questions, but I'll try to answer them based on the bible. It all goes back to the beginning, when Adam and Eve were in the Garden of Eden. (Read Genesis chapter 2 and 3 in the bible.) God told Adam and Eve that they could eat the fruit of any tree of the garden except from the tree of the knowledge of good and evil. He told them that if they ate the fruit of that tree, they would surely die. Well, Satan came along in the form of a serpent and tempted Eve. He told her that if she ate of the fruit, she would not surely die, as God had said, but that she would become wise like God. Eve listened to Satan, rather than God, and ate of the tree of the knowledge of good and evil. She not only ate of the tree herself, she gave the fruit to her husband, who ate it also.

When Adam and Eve turned away from God, and listened to Satan, sin, sickness, and death came into the world. Before that, everything was perfect. Nothing died. No one got sick and there weren't any problems.

But, why did God allow Adam and Eve to make a bad decision like that? Why didn't he stop them?

Well, God wants us to obey him because we love him – not because he forces us to obey him. He doesn't want us to be his puppets on a string. Think about it. Would you want a husband or wife to stay with you only because he/she had no choice? Of course not; you'd want them to stay because they love you. Well God doesn't want us to love and obey him because we are forced to. He gives us free choice. And that's the problem. Because he gives us free choice to do what we want, we often choose to rebel against God's protective commands. If God removed all evil and suffering, he would have to eliminate all human imperfection and force us to live without sinning. We would become robots, and have no free will.

When Adam and Eve chose to listen to Satan instead of God, they created havoc in the world. Well, why do we have to pay for their mistake? I used to wonder that, and then I realized that we are all imperfect, and each one of us would have made the same decision. It's so much easier to follow Satan than to follow God.

Satan wants to steal, kill and destroy, and he's doing a good job of that. The world is in a very bad condition today. We've made it that way by not putting God first. But, take heart! God is still in control. He sent his Son, Jesus to die on the cross for us, so that we might live forever in heaven with him. He's done his part. Our part is to accept Christ and live a life that is pleasing to God. We can make this world a better place by putting God first in our lives. It doesn't mean that when we do that everything will be perfect, but we will have God to depend upon. And do remember that we are not perfect ourselves, and God knows that. What he expects from us is that we love him with all of our hearts and try to please him. The Holy Spirit has been given to us, to help us. He will watch over us and get us through the bad times.

Faithfulness to God doesn't guarantee that a person's life will be free from suffering. It doesn't mean that when we are faithful that everything will be perfect. It does mean that we will have God to depend upon when troubles come.

# How Can I Forgive Those Who've Hurt Me?

They say that when life gives you lemons, make lemonade. It's an easy thing to say, but doing it is very difficult. Making lemonade often requires forgiving those who have hurt us. But should we forgive those who don't say they're sorry? If we forgive someone who has done something bad to us, aren't we helping them to continue doing it? Should we forgive everyone unconditionally? Are there times we should not forgive? Is there some evil that's too great to forgive?

I struggled with these questions for years. I forgave and forgot the evil done to me, only to have the person repeat it over and over again. I felt like a doormat, and it hurt. For a long while I thought that I should only forgive the person if they came to me and said they were sorry. But there are some people who will never do that. And that was the case with the person who continued to hurt me. So, they never said they were sorry, and I kept feeling guilty because I didn't forgive them. But then, as I was reading my bible one day, I had one of those 'ah-ha!' moments. When Jesus was on the cross, he prayed, "Father, forgive them, for they know not what they do." This prayer was for us, even though we weren't born yet. He prayed for us because we were the reason he was on the cross. It was our sin that placed him there. We hadn't said we were sorry, and yet he prayed that God would forgive us.

Also, the "Our Father" teaches us that we must forgive others in order to be forgiven:

"Our Father in heaven, hallowed be your name, your kingdom come, your will be done, on earth as it is in heaven. Give us today, our daily bread. Forgive us our debts, as we have forgiven our debtors. And lead us not into temptation, but deliver us from the evil one. For yours is the kingdom, and the power and the glory forever, amen."

As you can see in the prayer above, we need to forgive others so God can forgive us. We all sin – every one of us. So, how can we not forgive someone else's sin against us?

If your dad left you at some point in your life, I'm sure that you've been hurt badly by that. You needed him and he just wasn't there. Maybe you don't see any good reason for him leaving you like that. Or, maybe he was there and he wasn't a good father to you. You're hurt and you're angry. Who can blame you?

But, all the bitterness that you keep inside of you will only hurt *you*. It's important to forgive him for leaving you, for hurting you. Is it difficult? Yes! Can you do it? Yes! You may say, "But I don't feel like forgiving him!" I understand that. I've been there. Forgiveness doesn't begin with a feeling. It's an act of the will. You just have to decide to do it. And when you do, you will feel a wonderful freedom that will release you from that bitterness.

In her book, "Tramp for the Lord" Corrie Ten Boom, a Dutch Christian, tells of the atrocities she and her sister suffered in a concentration camp. They experienced near starvation and terrible cruelty from the guards. Her sister eventually died there in that concentration camp. After the war, Corrie returned to Holland to write books and do charitable works for the Lord. She spoke in a church in Munich, Germany about

God's forgiveness. Afterwards, much to her surprise and horror, she came face to face with the cruelest guard from the concentration camp.

All of a sudden, the memories flooded back to Corrie and she was again back in that concentration camp. She froze when she saw him. She could see that he did not remember her. He told her that he had been a guard in Ravensbruck, and had since become a Christian. He said he knew that God had forgiven him for what he had done, but he wanted to ask for her forgiveness also. "Will you forgive me?" he said, holding out his hand.

Put yourself in her position. What would you have done? This man had done evil things to you, your sister, and your people. Corrie struggled with forgiving him. She knew that Jesus would have her do it, but her hand wouldn't move to take the guard's hand. She prayed, "Jesus, help me!"

That's something that we can do when we have a hard time forgiving someone. We can ask the Lord for help. When Corrie asked for help, she received the strength she needed. She took the guard's hand and said, "I forgive you, Brother!"

If Corrie could forgive like that – if she could forgive such atrocities, can't we do the same? If Jesus could forgive on the cross as he suffered such pain, can't we do the same? Impossible to do? Yes, in our own strength. But with God's help, all things are possible!

# How God Can Become Your Greatest Dad

John 3:16 says, "For God so loved the world that he gave his only begotten Son that whosoever believes in him should not perish but have everlasting life." That means that God loves everyone so much that he allowed his son to die for us. God's son, Jesus, died for our sins so that we can be saved. When we accept Jesus as Savior, we become a child of God. It's so easy to become God's child and yet it's the most important thing that you can do. It will change your life!

Do you know that Jesus left all the riches of heaven to come to earth just to save you from your sins? He died on the cross for you. He would have done that for you even if you were the only one on earth. That's how much he loves you. And the way that we can show Jesus our love for him is to accept him into our hearts, love him and live for him.

Here's how to become a child of God:

1. John 3:16 tells us that God loves everyone and wants each one to become a member of his family.

2. Romans 3:23 and James 4:17 tell us that sin separates us from God. <u>Everyone</u> has sinned and needs forgiveness. Sin is disobeying God in any way.

3. Romans 6:23, Romans 5:8 and Peter 2:24 tell us that the punishment for sin is separation from God. This is spiritual death. But Jesus took our punishment for sin by dying on the cross for us.

4. Romans 6:23 and I John 1:9 tell us that salvation is free, it's a gift; we cannot buy it. We simply ask forgiveness for our sins and receive the gift of salvation. You can do this right now. Just pray and ask God to forgive you for your sins. Tell God that you believe Jesus died for your sins, and that you want to become a child of God.

5. Romans 10:9 says that after we accept salvation through faith, we need to tell others that we have received Jesus as Savior.

If you have done this, and you really, truly meant it, you are now a child of God. You now have the greatest dad as your father. Welcome to God's family! Now, go tell somebody! Tell somebody who will understand the things of God. And if you don't have a good, bible-believing church, find one. Start reading your Bible and praying to the Lord. He's interested in every part of your life, so include him in it. Tell him all your problems; let him help you. And remember, he loves you, and wants the best for you!

***Behold what manner of love the Father has bestowed on us, that we should be called children of God!***
***1 John 3:1***

# A Letter from Your Heavenly Father To You

My dear child, I want you to know that I love you, and I want to be a father to you, if you'll only let me. I wait for you with open arms. My greatest wish is for you to let me guide you and show you the way to live your life. I will take away your sin, and give you a new beginning. I wish to be there for you when you have problems. Share them with me, and I will help you carry them. I will not take you out of your problems, since problems are instrumental in helping you grow. I will, however, help you carry your burdens, and be right beside you through it all.

When you need someone to talk to, I will always be there for you. Just call on me, and I will listen. If you trust me, I will provide for your needs. I will not always give you everything you want because some things will harm you, but I will give you what you need. Lean on me, my dear child, and I will take you through the tough times. When you feel lonely, remember that I am there with you. I will never abandon you. If you follow my teachings, I will make you into a Godly person who needs not be ashamed. You will be able to go through life and not be afraid, for I am with you always, even to the end of the earth. Read my word, dear child, and it will show you how to live a Godly life. Stay close to me by conversing with me as you go through your day. I will help you through life's problems.

I love you, my child, and I will never forsake you. I sent my Son to die for you to take away your sin. If you were the only person in the whole world, I would still have sent my Son to die for you. That's how much I love you. You say that you have no father? I'm here to tell you that I will be your dad.

With Love,
Your Heavenly Father

# Famous People Who Grew Up Without a Father in the Home

U.S. Pres. George Washington

U.S. Pres. Thomas Jefferson

U.S. Pres. James Monroe

U.S. Pres. Andrew Jackson

U.S. Pres. Rutherford B. Hayes

U.S. Pres. James A. Garfield

U.S. Pres. Grover Cleveland

U.S. Pres. Herbert Hoover

U.S. Pres. Gerald Ford

U.S. Pres. William Jefferson Clinton

U.S. Pres. Barack Obama

George Washington Carver

Nathanial Hawthorne

Jackie Robinson

Benjamin Rush

Mark Twain

Booker T. Washington

Queen Elizabeth I

Nelson Mandela

Sir Isaac Newton

Leonardo Da Vinci

Maya Angelou

Jane Austin

Willa Cather

Mary Higgins Clark

Bill Cosby

Roald Dahl

Robert Frost

Sophia Loren

Willie Nelson

Shaquille O'Neal

Gov. Deval Laurdine Patrick

Wolfgang Puck

Raphael

Sacajawea

J.R. R. Tolkien

Leo Tolstoy

Queen Victoria

William Wordsworth

# Afterword

Many tears were shed in the writing of this book – tears of the contributors, as well as my own. It was almost as difficult for me to hear these stories, as it was for those who told them. My life has changed considerably since writing this book. I have a greater empathy for others, now that I've been given a glimpse into the burdens that people carry around with them. In the past, I would see people laughing and joking, with big smiles on their faces, and think they lived happy, carefree lives. But it is only when one hears the stories of what they've been through, that one realizes the heartache that exists within.

It was an emotional experience for these people to tell their stories to me. It brought back memories which they had hidden away and thought never to uncover. But after they shared their heartache and pain, each one declared to me that it was cathartic, and that they were glad that they did it. They were also hopeful that the telling of their stories would help others to get through bad times without a father. I thank them for their courage, and willingness to open their lives to us.

Life without a father creates a void which people strive a lifetime to fill. Only God can *perfectly* fill this void, and all one has to do is ask him.